LIGHTHOUSE
CONVERSATIONS

Being a Beacon for Teens

Jennifer Ollis Blomqvist

ISBN 978-91-987005-0-3 (paperback)
ISBN 978-91-987005-1-0 (ebook)
ISBN 978-91-987005-2-7 (UK paperback)
ISBN 978-91-987005-3-4 (UK e-book)

First Edition: June 2021

The author of this book has made every effort to use sources believed to be reliable to provide information that is accurate and compatible with the standards generally accepted at the time of publication.

However, with respect to the possibility of human error or changes in behavioural, mental health, or medical sciences, the author or any other person who has been involved in the preparation or publication of this work, are not responsible for any errors or omissions in the text. The author is not responsible for any special, consequential, or exemplary damages resulting, in whole or in part, from the readers' use of, or reliance on, the information contained in this book. Readers are encouraged to confirm the information contained in this book with other sources. The author has no responsibility for the persistence or accuracy of URLs for external or third-party Internet websites referred to in this publication and does not guarantee that any content on such websites is, or will remain, accurate or appropriate.

Cover design by Victor Orozco
Interior layout and eBook design by Amit Dey
Interior graphics by Natalie Lake and Jennifer Ollis Blomqvist
Edited by Robyn MacMillan

Jennifer Ollis Blomqvist
NovoVia Consulting
jennifer@novovia.se
www.novovia.se

The book's additional resources can be downloaded at https://en.novovia.se/bookresources.

This book is printed on demand, eliminating the negative environmental impact of printing large qualities of books that might go unsold and contribute to waste. Paper used is sourced from sustainable forests and ink used does not contain any animal products.

PREFACE

I have extensive work experience with adults struggling with mental illness, addictions, and criminal behaviour. I have also had the honour of witnessing these adults make life changes, big or small. Often from an early age, my clients struggled with their mental health, skipped school, partied, drank and/or did drugs, hung out with the "wrong" crowd, and got into trouble with the law. Their destructive behaviour escalated during their teenage years and by the time I had the chance to work with them, the downward spiral was often already out of control. This downward spiral is exactly what I want to prevent! With this book, I am inviting you, the reader, to intervene early and help teens showing signs of troubling behaviour.

Lighthouse Conversations gives adults the tools!

We have the chance, responsibility, and an important role in guiding teens and this book is aimed at supporting adults to do just that. Whether you are a family member, teacher, counsellor, coach, or other important adult in a teen's life, this book is written to help you feel confident to better support teenagers, improve your relationship with them by communicating effectively, and prevent problems before they escalate.

The name *Lighthouse Conversations. Being a Beacon for Teens.*

Our role and responsibility as adults in the lives of teens is very similar to that of a lighthouse. Regardless of the weather, a lighthouse stands firmly on the shore guiding boats to safety. This book is a road map for having guided conversations with teens using Motivational Interviewing (MI). MI is a proven counselling approach that uses a compassionate and collaborative conversational style to strengthen self-motivation and commitment to change (Miller & Rollnick, 2013). We are the lighthouse on the shore, and our roles and responsibilities are to guide teens through one of the most challenging and wonderful times of their lives. Join me in being a beacon for teens.

Lindome, Sweden
Jennifer Ollis Blomqvist, BSc, MSW, Cognitive Behavioural Coach
MI-trainer, Member of MINT (Motivational Interviewing Network of Trainers)

ACKNOWLEDGEMENTS

I truly am fortunate to have had so many kind and supportive people during this journey. My amazing and knowledgeable team happily offered hours of their time for discussions and brainstorming meetings. My creative and awesome brother Jeff Ollis, my talented graphic designer and friend Natalie Lake, my incredible branding and marketing team Kim Marie McKernan and Victor Orozco, are just a few of the people who made this book possible. A special thank you goes out to Robyn MacMillian and her huge heart for supporting me in my writing process and for her generosity while editing this book.

A big shout out goes to "MINTies" all over the world. I am honoured and grateful to be a part of a community that shares my love for and dedication to MI. Together we create exercises and training material to spread high-quality MI to others, many of which are included in this book. A big thank you to my cheerleaders, Karolina Edler for her inspiration, strength, wisdom, and empathy throughout this entire process, and Kate Watson for her reassurance and for having my back. A special thank you goes out to Richard Rutschman who happily and willingly read my manuscript while on his vacation in Mexico. It meant a great deal to receive Richard's valuable and positive feedback, as his work with MI in schools has fueled my own motivation for spreading MI in the education system, with parents and caregivers, and with teens.

Last, but not least, I could not have done this without the love, encouragement, and support of my family. I want to thank my children, Ian and Emelie, for helping me become the adult and parent that I am, accepting me as an "MI Nerd," and showing patience in my many MI inspired conversations. I am especially grateful for their voices in the audio files and their willingness to use some of our personal stories in this book. My husband, Magnus Blomqvist, has been my rock during this process. He believed in me, lent me his strength, and pushed me when I doubted myself. I am grateful to my mother, Sharon Ollis, for her love and support, especially in increasing my Dad's inner motivation to help me when it faded. I guess I know where I get that from! A great big thank you goes out to my dad, Gerald Ollis, for spending hours and hours of his time discussing the content, challenging and encouraging me, editing my Swenglish, and even learning from the material. If it wasn't for you Dad, I never would have taken the step to actually turn what I had into this book.

Thank you!!
Jennifer Ollis Blomqvist

TABLE OF CONTENTS

Chapter 1: Introduction   1

Part One: The Basics   9

Chapter 2: Being a Teen   11

Chapter 3: The Relational Foundation   14

Chapter 4: Communication   21

Chapter 5: Motivation   34

Chapter 6: Eliciting Motivation   48

Part Two: Delving Deeper   77

Chapter 7: Communicate using EOE (Explore - Offer – Explore)   79

Chapter 8: Step 1: Explore (E)   86

Chapter 9: Step 2: Offer (O)   113

Chapter 10: Step 3: Explore (E)   143

Part Three: Self-Care   153

Chapter 11: Importance of Self-Care   155

Chapter 12: Increase Positivity in Your Life   158

Chapter 13: Breathing and Relaxation Techniques   164

Chapter 14: Coping with Strong Feelings   172

Chapter 15: Being Kind to Yourself   178

Chapter 16: Social and Emotional Self-Care   181

Chapter 17: Developing Helpful Thinking Patterns   186

Chapter 18: Conclusion   193

Appendix   195

References   199

Chapter 1

INTRODUCTION

"Courage is what it takes to stand up and speak; courage is also what it takes to sit down and listen."

— Winston Churchill

*H*ave you heard this before? Can you relate to this kind of communication with a teen in your circle? If so, you are not alone!

Communication between people can sometimes feel overwhelming and challenging, and at the same time, it is so incredibly important. Good communication involves listening to understand another person's perspective alongside effectively getting across what you want to say. It is a two-way street. Yet, despite our best efforts and intentions, our communications can still become muddled or misunderstood.

Communication with teens can be thought of as a road full of potholes. Sometimes, we may be aware of the potholes and have time to change and adapt our route. Other times, we can see the potholes in the distance and are able to slow down, or carefully plan our path accordingly. Our reflexes may be quick enough to avoid a large pothole, only to run into a smaller one instead. All this is very common, and even normal!

Communication with teens is also rewarding, and good communication will strengthen your relationship with them. *Lighthouse Conversations* focuses on communicating effectively with a teen you know and interact with while increasing their inner motivation for change. Imagine driving down a road with potholes, where the potholes represent communication issues with a teen. This book is about avoiding as many of these "potholes" as possible. It will also help you repair any damage caused by unintentionally hitting a "pothole".

After reading this book, you will have learned about:

- Your "listening hat" and how you can improve your listening skills to better understand a teen and how to get your message across when needed.

- How you can develop and enrich your relationship using Motivational Interviewing (MI) to develop and strengthen a collaborative partnership, communicate acceptance, demonstrate compassion, and focus on a teen's strengths.

- The definition of "autonomy" and how you can support a teen's autonomy through constructive conversation.

- A new 3-step framework to communicate more effectively with a teen and to deliver your message to ensure it gets across (Explore - Offer - Explore).

- Conversational tools used to communicate more effectively with teens, including questions, reflections, summaries, affirmations, "asking for permission."
- How to influence a teen's openness and motivation to receive and internalize your message.
- How to care for yourself so that you can effectively communicate with teens.

After reading this book, you will be better able to:

- Learn about the processes that support conversations with a teen in your circle, which will help you feel more comfortable hearing about that teen's perspective. This book provides you with helpful strategies and tools to communicate constructively with a teen.
- Recognize your own strengths in all current, successful conversations.
- Feel confident with the tools that are provided to help you collaborate actively with a teen, communicate constructively, and enrich your relationship.
- Understand the importance of creating an atmosphere of acceptance, showing empathy, and communicating compassion for the teen's point of view. You will be better able to show understanding for the teen's perspective and demonstrate effective listening skills.
- Express your expectations and desires, as well as deliver your messages constructively with the help of I-messages and a Three-part Communication Model.
- Learn more about successful strategies for enhancing your own well-being and taking care of yourself, such as increasing positivity in your life and nourishing your relationships and interests.

- Notice, identify, analyze, and modify your own thoughts, feelings, and behaviours, as well as use breathing and relaxation exercises to improve your well-being.
- Learn some strategies used for coping with powerful emotions.

The material in this book consists of theory sections, everyday examples, audio files and videos, images, diagrams, and other helpful tools to make the content meaningful and easier to understand. All downloadable material and audio files can be found at https://en.novovia. se/bookresources.

Throughout the book, there will be several opportunities for you to reflect on the material and the themes that are presented. Together with a teen, there are plenty of conversational activities for you to engage in, as well as exercises to help you incorporate the content into your daily life. After each exercise, there are questions that are designed for you to reflect on to promote your learning and understanding of the content within this book.

As this may be a new way of communicating for both you and the teen, some exercises and activities may feel unnatural or unfamiliar in the beginning. Please don't worry, this is completely normal! This way of communicating takes practice, effort, and time. You may occasionally make mistakes but that is also to be expected! Making mistakes is part of the process and the most important thing is that you are trying.

So, hang in there!

The Book Layout

Part One focuses on building the foundation for communicating effectively with teens while increasing their inner motivation for change. You'll find:

- In Chapter 2, a brief introduction to the development of the adolescent brain to help you understand the biological reasons for some teenage behaviours.

- In Chapter 3, a focus on the importance of a positive relationship with a teen and practical exercises in how you can achieve that. This chapter also provides practical exercises for you to further develop your relationship with that teen by enriching your conversations with them and understanding what they value.

- In Chapter 4, an exploration of communication and listening with empathy. This chapter discusses "roadblocks to listening" and how these roadblocks affect your communication with teens. There are reflection and practical exercises for you to understand, practice, and enhance your own listening skills.

- In Chapter 5, an introduction to the concept of motivation and a teen's motivational language, or "change talk." This chapter will help you understand the driving forces behind a teen's actions and teach you to explore their motivation for change in conversation.

- In Chapter 6, an introduction to eliciting motivation in conversations with teenagers using Motivational Interviewing (MI). This chapter explains MI's communication style and spirit as an effective way to discuss change with teens while supporting and promoting their autonomy. It briefly introduces the tool EOE (Explore-Offer-Explore) used to both explore a teen's point of view while respectfully delivering your message to that teen.

In Part Two of the book, we dive deeper into the different conversational tools used to convey MI's communication and listening style, while increasing their motivation for change and supporting their autonomy. Part Two includes example situations and several practical exercises to help you develop and apply the theoretical concepts in your own interactions with a teen. You'll find:

- In Chapter 7, a comprehensive description of the tool EOE (Explore-Offer-Explore) and how you can affect a teen's openness to communicate with you and receive your delivered message.

- In Chapter 8, a detailed explanation of the tool EOE's first step – Step 1: Explore (E). The chapter includes the essential active listening skills needed when exploring a teen's point of view before offering your own perspective. Conversational tools, such as affirming a teen, asking open-ended questions, and forming reflections are illustrated with examples. Exercises to help you practice and apply these tools in current conversations with teens are presented.

- In Chapter 9, a description of Step 2: Offer (O) including helpful ideas for conveying your message to a teen in an effective and respectful way. The chapter provides several tips for packaging your message to increase a teen's openness to take in what you have to say, all while supporting their autonomy at the same time. In this step, I-messages and a structured Three-Part Communication Model are presented to support you in respectfully delivering your message while being mindful of how your message may be received by the teen.

- In Chapter 10, a thorough explanation of Step 3: Explore (E) includes the importance and necessity of checking the teen's understanding of your message and getting feedback from them.

Part Three focuses on the importance of self-care when communicating with a teen and provides some helpful strategies, exercises, tools, and techniques that can help you take care of yourself. You'll find:

- In Chapter 11, a general discussion about self-care and a reflection exercise to help you determine what recharges your batteries.

- In Chapter 12, a brief introduction to the importance of increasing positivity in your daily life as a way of taking care of yourself. This chapter touches on how kindness and positivity feed off each other.

- In Chapter 13, examples and exercises introducing breathing and relaxation techniques to help you manage the effects of stress on your mind and body.

- In Chapter 14, a brief introduction to our basic human emotions and how you can better cope with overwhelming feelings. In this chapter we look at the idea of emotion surfing and its impact on coping with strong emotions.

- In Chapter 15, a brief introduction to the benefits of being kind to yourself by being self-accepting and self-compassionate, discovering your positive personal attributes, and affirming yourself.

- In Chapter 16, be encouraged to engage in meaningful leisure time and be invited to nourish the relationships that are important to you and that give you positive energy. This chapter also includes asking for help as an important aspect of social and emotional self-care.

- In Chapter 17, a basic introduction to how your thoughts about a specific situation are connected to and affect both your feelings and behaviour, otherwise known as Cognitive Behavioural Therapy (CBT). This chapter helps you become aware of your helpful and "unhelpful" thoughts, tackle your "unhelpful" thoughts, and challenge or replace your "unhelpful" thoughts.

Image Directory

 This symbol warns that you may need to be more aware or observant when communicating with a teen. A cautionary "something *to think about*..." or "something to be *aware off*..."

 You will see this image when a suggestion or tip is offered, in reference to, what is being presented.

 This image indicates reflective exercises on the content, a recent conversation with a teen, or a mindset that you may have discovered in yourself.

Practical exercises throughout the book are symbolized by this "driver in training" car. Just like getting your Learner's Permit where you are required to practice your driving skills before taking your test and obtaining your Driver's License. The more you practice your driving skills, the better driver you become and the same applies to your communication skills. The more you practice the conversational tools presented in this book, the more skilled you will become in using these during your interactions with a teen.

Now you are in pole position, it's time for you to get ready to start driving down the road with potholes.

Part One

The Basics

Chapter 2

BEING A TEEN

Exercise: Being a Teen

 Objective: To look back and remember your own teenage years.

Instructions: Think back to when you were a teen, and then reflect using the questions below.

- What was it like being a teen?
- What sorts of thoughts about yourself and other people in your life did you have during those years?
- What was important to you?
- Which people were important to you?
- What do you remember about your interactions with adults during your teenage years?

The Adolescent Brain

A LOT happens, both physically and emotionally, as a child develops into an adult. A few years ago, I attended a conference session about the development of the adolescent brain. The lecturer, Dr. Bobby Smyth, described the development of a teen's brain using an excellent metaphor which I will try to explain here (Smyth, 2017).

Dr. Smyth compared childhood to a small car. The car's frame, engine, and brakes are smaller. It is easier to drive because it is small. The small car has everything needed during childhood and matches the developmental age of the "driver."

 Because of an adult's experience, maturity, and enhanced skill levels, adulthood can be compared to a larger and better car. Think of adulthood as a cool, sporty Ferrari with a powerful engine and "big" brakes able to handle the Ferrari engine's power.

 Evolution is not very kind to teens. They have it tough; they are caught in the middle of the transitional process from small car to Ferrari. On the outside, teens seem all grown up but, on the inside, they are still "adults in training." Evolution has provided teens with a Ferrari body, including the powerful engine, but with tiny brakes from the small car! Consider this, the braking distance for the Ferrari with the small brakes is much, much further. The whole teen, including their brain, is a work in progress and it can be useful to see a teen as an "apprentice" (Smyth, B., 2017). As a result, it is normal for teens to experiment in risky behaviour, seek excitement, and be strongly influenced by their emotions.

The human brain develops from the "bottom up" meaning that the first part of the brain to develop is the brain stem and amygdala (Jensen, 2015). The amygdala is the area responsible for instinct, impulses, emotions, and aggressive behaviour. Once developed, the pre-frontal cortex in the frontal lobe balances the amygdala's responses with common-sense, logic, and responsibility. The pre-frontal cortex, however, is not fully developed until at least 24 years of age (Young, 2021). The pre-frontal cortex is responsible for comprehension, decision-making, considering consequences, planning, problem-solving, and handling strong emotions (Jensen, 2015).

Therefore, teens engaging in risky behaviour are largely influenced by the imbalance between the fully developed amygdala and the underdeveloped pre-frontal cortex. Also, as the pre-frontal cortex develops more slowly, the "brakes" that control emotions and impulses also develop at a much slower rate (Dolgin, 2014, Young, 2021).

Chapter Wrap-Up

The teenage years can be challenging due to the development of the teen's brain and the physical and emotional impacts that has on the teen. This chapter considered:

- The understanding that the brain develops from the bottom up and how this development affects communication with a teen in your circle.
- The part of the brain responsible for important functions such as decision-making, considering consequences, and problem-solving (the pre-frontal cortex) is the last to develop. This helps to explain teenage behaviours, such as lack of impulse control or emotional outbursts.

DODGE IT!	TRY IT!
The "Blame Game"- Blaming the teen for evolution's decision.	Show **ACCEPTANCE** during this turbulent time.
Getting caught up in an emotional storm.	**Lend your brakes.** Remember that a teen is not yet "wired" the same as an adult.

Chapter 3

THE RELATIONAL FOUNDATION

A positive relationship is the ultimate goal when communicating with teens, especially when it comes to talking about issues, they find difficult to articulate. A positive relationship is needed to understand each other's perspectives, to get across an important message, and to sow the seeds of change which will lead to a better situation for all. A trusting and safe relationship is needed for a teen to feel accepted for who they are and for them to feel that the adults around them value them as a unique individual. It is important for a teen to feel actively engaged in your relationship so that they do not believe that adults are the only ones able to make decisions. Adults around them must show a genuine interest in a teen's life and the relationship must reflect mutual respect and acceptance.

A positive and enriched relationship is the foundation of Motivational Interviewing (MI). Getting to know a teen as a unique individual, for example, what they are passionate about, what is important to them, their qualities, strengths and positive resources, their way of thinking and perspectives, is a fundamental necessity to be able to communicate about important and serious or difficult issues.

It is now time for the first exercise which encourages you to reflect on your current conversational skills.

Exercise: A Positive Conversation

Objective: To reflect over a positive conversation you have had with a person or a teen.

Instructions: Think back to a recent conversation that you have had with a person or a teen that you thought was positive.

- What reactions by the other person indicated to you that the conversation went well?
- What did you do to make it a positive conversation?
- How can you incorporate this in your everyday interactions with a teen?

Communication, at its core, is an interaction between people. It includes both listening to another person's perspective *and* clearly delivering your message. This book will provide you with tips on how to improve your listening skills and how to constructively deliver your message to a teen, all while increasing their inner motivation for change.

Exercise: Conversing with Teens

Objective: To reflect on your current communication skills during a conversation with an important teen in your circle.

Instructions: The next time a teen opens up to you about something, whatever that may be, listen attentively. Following that conversation, spend approximately 10 minutes reflecting on the thoughts, feelings, and actions you experienced. Use the following questions to guide your reflection.

- How was your experience of the conversation? How did it make you feel?

- Who talked the most during the conversation?
- What important things did you hear the teen say?

 Focusing on what *you* are going to say in a conversation makes it harder to listen to what the teen is telling you. This may cause you to miss what the teen is trying to communicate to you.

Develop and Enrich your Relationship

A good relationship is characterized by a sense of warmth, security, and positivity. It is also formed by setting clear expectations and boundaries that are conveyed with respect. A good relationship is needed for a teen to feel comfortable and safe talking to you about important or difficult subjects. A teen should be confident that you are a reliable and stable adult who is ready, willing, and able to stand your ground even when it feels tough for the both of you.

It takes a positive atmosphere and a lot of time having conversations with teens to get to know what makes them "tick" and to form a good, positive relationship with them. As a parent, or another important adult in a teen's circle, there is always more that you can learn about the teen in front of you. Presented below are two ways to further develop and enrich your relationship with an important teen in your life.

Exercise: Enriching a Conversation with a Teen

 **Objective:** To talk about topics with a teen that you may not usually talk about.

Instructions: Download the conversational cards at https://en.novovia.se/bookresources. Print and cut out the conversational cards. Take turns drawing a card and asking/ answering the questions written on each card. The questions on the conversational cards are also provided below.

- If you were to give away something meaningful, what would you give, and to whom?
- What three people (living or deceased) would you like to invite for supper, and why?
- What warms your heart?
- What would you like to invent and why?
- What would you like to have the courage to do?
- What do you value the most in other people?
- What is the best thing that has happened to you in a long time?
- What is meaningful to you?
- What is most important to you right now?
- What do you wish for the most, right now?

Self-reflection

- How do you feel the conversation went?
- What new things did you learn about the teen?
- What important things did you hear the teen say?
- How can you incorporate this in your everyday interactions with the teen?

What Teens Value

One way to get to know a teen on an enhanced level is to identify, explore, and discuss their values. Core values are what we care the most about, drive us to reach our goals and "guide how we perceive and behave in the world" (Miller, 2018, p.70). They are the beliefs and opinions that we stand for and strive to achieve. For example, these could be, independence, autonomy, justice, integrity, family, leisure (Miller & Rollnick, 2013). They also help us advocate for ourselves and others, prioritize in our lives, and guide how we behave in different situations.

It is key to learn about and discuss the things that are most important to a teen. When you know what is important to a teen, you can appreciate their "internal frame of reference" and understand the reasons why they act as they do in certain situations (Miller & Rollnick, 2013, p.74). Discussing values with teens further promotes engagement in your collaboration, increases teens' inner drive to proceed forward, and gives you an insight into their thoughts, feelings, and perspectives.

 During a conversation with a teen about core values, if the teen does not understand the meaning of the word "value," it can be helpful to talk to them more generally, about "what is important to them."

Exercise: Explore a Teen's Values

 **Objective:** To identify and explore what a teen values.

Instructions: Listen carefully, identify, and explore what a teen values. Ask the following questions and feel free to summarize what is important to the teen.

- What are the current priorities in your life? In what way are they important to you?
- What do you think is important to have in a friend, in a sport, or at school? What makes that important to you? What do these things mean to you?
- Tell me what you care the most about in the world. What matters the most to you?
- What would you say are the rules you live by? What do you try to live up to?
- What do you hope your life to look like by next year?
- How do you live your values?

- How do you show that _____ is important in your everyday life?
- In what situations it is easy/difficult for you to express how that _____ is important to you?

Self-reflection

- How do you feel the conversation went?
- What new things did you learn about the teen?
- What important things did you hear the teen say?
- How can you incorporate this in your everyday interactions with the teen?

Exercise: Explore a Teen's Values Using Structured Value Cards

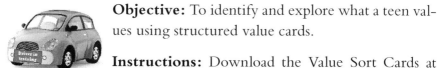

Objective: To identify and explore what a teen values using structured value cards.

Instructions: Download the Value Sort Cards at https://en.novovia.se/bookresources. Print and cut out the value cards. Allow the teen to sort through the value cards and choose the ones that they deem important to them. The blank cards are provided for the teen to suggest values of their own. After the teen has chosen the cards, discuss each value card one at a time. Listen carefully to the teen and ask questions to further understand what the teen is communicating to you. Summarize the key points of what the teen has said and thank them for the conversation. If you need to, you may use some of the following questions to get you started.

- What is the reason that _____ is important to you?
- How would it be noticeable to someone else that _____ is important to you?

- How did _____ become important to you?
- When does _____ become extra important for you? When does _____ become less important to you?
- If you were to place the cards in order from least important to most important, how would you place them? What are your reasons for choosing that order?
- How happy are you with that arrangement? Is there any value card you would like to move to another spot?

Self-reflection

- How do you feel the conversation went?
- What new things did you learn about the teen?
- What important things did you hear the teen say?
- How can you incorporate this in your everyday interactions with the teen?

Chapter Wrap-Up

A positive and mutually respectful relationship is the foundation for good communication with anyone, especially a teen. This chapter covered:

- How a teen needs to be actively engaged in your relationship and shown that their point of view is important to you.
- How to develop and enrich your relationship with a teen.
- The importance of deepening your conversations with teens by learning what a teen in your circle values and how this shapes their outlook on situations.

DODGE IT!	TRY IT!
A *mainly* adult perspective.	Establishing a positive relationship with a strong teen focus. Discuss a teen's values.

Chapter 4

COMMUNICATION

The Purpose of Listening

"We have two ears and one mouth, and we should use them proportionally"

— **Susan Cain,**
Quiet: The Power of Introverts
in a World That Can't Stop Talking

*H*ave you ever had a conversation with a teen that ended in them suddenly becoming frustrated and telling you that you are not listening to them? You are shocked and baffled and don't understand because you were so engaged in the conversation. I mean you were asking questions, giving suggestions, providing solutions, and really trying to help...or?

You meant well and thought you were being kind and helpful by coming up with solutions for the teen's problems. However, coming up with solutions does not necessarily mean that you really listened to the teen's story and/or *understood* the teen's perspective. *"Helping"* for you means *"solving"* the teen's problems. You need to consider that focusing on finding

FIXER

solutions does not necessarily communicate to the teen that you are interested in seeing the problem through their eyes or experiences.

This well-intentioned need to solve, or fix, a teen's problems is called the "righting-reflex" (Miller & Rollnick, 2013, p.5-6). The "righting-reflex" may surface because it bothers you to watch an important teen close to you struggle, and you are compelled to relieve your own discomfort by fixing it. In that moment, it is easier for you to put on your "fixer hat" and fix things quickly to save time and ease the suffering for you both.

In that moment, you may make it easier for the teen, but this also has some negative effects. Indirectly, you are conveying to the teen that they are unable to handle the situation themselves. Ultimately, what you have done is taken away the teen's responsibility for the problem. You have removed the option of working out the best solution and the possibility for them to grow and change. This urgent need to help, giving way to our "righting-reflex," or putting on our "fixer hat" is **not listening with empathy or listening with the intent to understand.**

Exercise: Wearing Your "Fixer Hat" During a Conversation

Objective: To reflect over a conversation or situation when your urgent need to help took over, your "righting-reflex" kicked in, or you put on your "fixer hat."

Instructions: Reflect over the following questions.

- What situation or situations triggered your "righting-reflex"?
- In what way have you unintentionally worn your "fixer hat" and taken over a conversation?
- What could you have done instead of putting on your "fixer hat"?
- When have you, on a previous occasion, been able to override your "righting-reflex"? How did you do it?

Meaning Well or Inhibiting

When talking with teens, we may intend to and think we are really listening to what they have to say. However, even though our motivation is to "help" the teen, we may end up doing something different. For example, offering solutions which has the opposite effect. It is important to reflect on the fact that being kind and "meaning well" may not translate into knowing what is best for a teen (Ortiz & Skoglund, 2017). Sometimes our kindness, although well-intentioned, can be misinterpreted with the teen believing we just do *not* get it. This affects communication negatively and inhibits the relationship.

Roadblocks to Listening

Listening is a very important part of communication with a teenager, but it can sometimes be the most difficult part. Because of this, it can be helpful to familiarize yourself with 12 common listener responses, or "roadblocks," that get in the way of good listening and block communication (Gordon, 2019).

1. **Giving Advice, Making Suggestions, Providing Solutions**

   Involves offering assistance to a teen when it is not asked for.

   > *How about…?*
   > *Have you thought about…?*
   > *What I would do is…*

2. **Ordering or Directing**

   Not giving the teen a choice by telling them what to do.

   > *Don't say that!*
   > *Do something about it.*
   > *Just stop it, OK?!*

3. Warning or Threatening

Including pointing out the risks or dangers of a teen's actions.

If you don't start listening to me, I am going to take away your phone privileges.

Don't you test me!

I'm warning you. You are going to get into trouble.

4. Moralizing or Preaching

Telling a teen what they should or ought to do, think, or feel.

You know...you really shouldn't do that...

You really ought to know better than that...

5. Persuading with Logic, Lecturing, Convincing

Providing reasons and teaching a teen a lesson.

Yes...but...

Come on...do it for me!

Well, of course the teacher doesn't like you when you act out in class every day!

Come on...you have to go to school. It'll feel better once you get there.

6. Judging, Criticizing, Blaming

Involves making judgements or evaluating a teen's thoughts, feelings, or behaviour.

You're not thinking clearly.

What were you thinking?

You are so selfish sometimes.

You got yourself into this position! It's your own fault.

7. Shaming, Ridiculing, Labelling, Name-calling

Involves making a teen feel silly or embarrassed by attaching a name or stereotype to what they are doing or saying.

You should be ashamed.

Don't be such a worrywart!

You're overreacting.

That really wasn't smart!

8. Interpreting or Analyzing

Focusing on your interpretation or explanation of what the teen is doing or saying.

Oh, really now. You are just tired.

You really didn't mean to say that.

I think what you really mean is…

I am sure that he/she didn't mean that…

9. Agreeing, Approving, Praising

Involves making evaluations and taking sides in an issue.

You are so right! Your teacher should have given you more time for the assignment.

Yep, that's what I would do.

You are such a good friend.

I agree with you. No one should be able to treat you like that.

Good job!

10. Reassuring, Sympathizing, Consoling

Talking a teen out of their feelings, minimizing their difficulties, and denying the seriousness of their problems.

Look on the bright side…

It's not that bad.

Don't worry, everything will look better after a good night's sleep.

There there…you poor thing.

11. Questioning or Probing

Asking questions to gather facts or pressing for more information, instead of listening.

Soooo……what do you think?

Didn't that make you mad?

And what did you do?

12. Distracting, Humouring, Changing the Subject

Diverting the teen away from what they are currently experiencing.

Can we discuss this another day?

Suck it up!

You know…..I forgot to tell you…

You know…I'm not very good at this….

That reminds me. We need to do…… instead.

When you want to *listen* to a teen's thoughts and perspectives, but you utilize these "roadblocks," they have serious consequences for the conversation and for your relationship. They tend to:

- Stop a teen from expressing how they are truly feeling.
- Interfere with the teen's ability to explore their own thoughts, feelings, and perspective.
- Communicate non-acceptance for the teen's perspective.
- Convey a desire for the teen to think, feel, or act differently than how they wish to respond.
- Indicate that you know best by placing an "expert hat" on your head.
- Signal that we are uncomfortable with hearing the teen's thoughts about their situation.

When communicating like this, teens will most likely react by shutting down, defending themselves, going quiet, or behaving in the opposite way of how we want them to. What we intended to achieve (an effective conversation) evoked the opposite result (an ineffective conversation). The focus switched from listening to and understanding the teen to formulating arguments and defending yourself.

Put simply, you have stopped listening to each other. An example where this happens is when sentences start with, *"yes, but..."* The word *"but"* silently erases what was said before and gives weight to what was said afterwards. This is a good example of roadblock no. 5 - Persuading with Logic, Lecturing, Convincing.

It is important to remember that these common listening responses often come from a good place and that they are not ALWAYS wrong. We mean well! It is just important to consider the purpose of your conversation with a teen. If you are intending to listen to understand a teen's perspective, then avoiding the above roadblocks are a necessity to allow the teen to express themselves freely.

Lighthouse Conversations provides many conversational tools and strategies to help you reach your communication goals with teens close to you, while avoiding as many roadblocks as possible.

Exercise: Your Own Listening

Objective: To explore, reflect, and enhance your knowledge of your own listening skills.

Instructions: Think back to a recent conversation that you have had with a person or teen that you thought was positive. Reflect on your listening skills by answering the following questions. If you are comfortable doing so, select someone in your circle and ask them to answer the following questions regarding your own listening skills.

- When am I good at listening? What do I do to show that I am listening?
- How do I show I am listening (i.e., body language and verbal cues)? What could I do to show I am listening?
- How important is it for me to improve my listening skills, on a scale from 0–10?
    - What makes it a _____ and not a lower number?
    - What would be needed to raise my number to a higher level?
- How confident am I that I *can* improve my listening skills, on a scale from 0-10?
    - What is it that makes it a _____ and not a lower number?
    - What would be needed to raise my number to a higher level?
- How ready am I to improve my listening skills, on a scale from 0-10?
    - What is it that makes it a _____ and not a lower number?
    - What would be needed to raise my number to a higher level?
- What do I do too much of, or too little of, in conversations with other people (when I try to listen)?
- What times am I better at listening?
- When do I find it particularly difficult to listen?

The Importance of Body Language While Listening

Communication consists of both verbal and non-verbal signals. Most communication is non-verbal, thereby you reveal more about your feelings, thoughts, and attitudes from your body language. What signals you send out during your communication, and how they are perceived by the teen are crucial to the conversation, and for your relationship. Your body language says more than words (Alberti & Emmons, 2017; Miller & Rollnick, 2013; Gordon, 2019).

Listening with Empathy

According to MI, empathy is a genuine and active interest in, or effort to, understand another person's inner world (Miller & Rollnick, 2013). Empathetic helping professionals are curious and use core conversational skills (such as open questions and reflections) to encourage their client to understand themselves by elaborating beyond what is necessary to merely follow the story (Miller & Rollnick, 2013; Miller, 2018). In this sense, empathy is *not* a personal attribute that an individual has or doesn't have. Empathy is a way of thinking and being and demonstrating it speaks to the helping professional's **attempts** to understand the other person's perspective.

Listening with empathy involves listening with the intent to understand. This can be accomplished using active listening skills which can be learned, improved, and perfected. Conveying empathy to a teen speaks to the efforts made to understand what it may be like to walk in that teen's shoes. Expressing empathy is being a curious and interested adult wanting to help a teen understand why they do what they do, react as they react, say what they say, think as they think, and feel as they feel.

It is, however, also important to be mindful and accept that actively *trying* or *attempting* to understand a teen's point of view does not automatically mean that you *will* be *able* to understand it. You might be able to get a general idea about a teen's inner frame of reference for example, but this may not be the full story. You may possibly *identify* with the teen because of similarities in your own past experiences. Or you might even be able to *sympathize with*, or *feel pity for,* a teen. But acquiring a general understanding for, identifying with, or sympathizing with, a teen is not the same as expressing empathy (Miller & Rollnick, 2013).

Conveying Empathy using Summaries

A summary is a conversational tool used to show a teen that you are striving to understand their point of view by really listening to what they are trying to say. In other words, summarizing shows the teen that you are listening with empathy.

Summarizing involves collecting what a teen has said and offering it back to them, as you would a bouquet of flowers. Summaries have different functions and can be used to:

- Tie things together at the end of a conversation (i.e., *"So, one thing you're telling me is that…"* or *"If I understand you correctly, you want to…"*).
- Link together what was said during different conversations (i.e., *"You feel really frustrated in social studies – like you don't understand what is expected of you. I remember you told me before about another assignment that felt unclear"*).
- Transition from one topic of conversation to another.
- Provide a "what else?" opportunity for the teen to fill in what you may have missed and invite the teen to further explore a topic (Miller & Rollnick, 2013).

Summaries include information that the teen has communicated through their words and body language. Summaries are beneficial because they allow the teen to hear and reflect upon what they have said during the conversation, and because they invite continued exploration of a topic.

As a guideline for talking with teens, summaries should be short (i.e., max 20 seconds) to focus solely on the teen's experience and capture the essence of what the teen has said during the conversation.

Helpful Steps to Enhance your Listening Skills

Discover your "Listening Hat"

1. Stop and think about your current intention for listening. Ask yourself: "*What should the purpose of my listening be right now?*"

2. Put aside *your* viewpoint or agenda and be present in the current conversation.

3. Be relaxed and calm.

Listening

1. Listen carefully to what the teen is saying.

2. Talk less than the teen.

3. Listen with curiosity. What does the teen mean?

4. Summarize what the teen has said. What did you hear the teen say? What do you think the teen is trying to communicate to you, but not yet verbalized?

Exercise: Listening

Objective: To explore and practice your listening skills, especially using summaries.

Instructions: Talk with a teen and explore their reasons for liking their leisure activities, work, or studies. Use the "Helpful Steps to Enhance your Listening," remember to summarize what the teen has said, and concentrate on having a good conversation. Feel free to use one of the following questions as a conversation starter.

- What five things could you not live without?
- What do you like about your work/leisure activities/studies?

If you are comfortable, try forming mini-summaries, or reflections, focusing on what the teen has said throughout the conversation. Provide a larger summary at the end of the conversation beginning with, "*So, you ......*"

 Remember that a summary includes what the teen has expressed in their own words, what you may hear but that the teen has not yet explicitly said, and what you read between the lines.. Feel free to rephrase if needed. At the end of your conversation, thank the teen for speaking with you.

Self-reflection

- How do you feel the conversation went?
- What new things did you learn about the teen?
- What important things did you hear the teen say?
- How can you incorporate this in your everyday interactions with the teen?

Chapter Wrap-Up

This chapter explored the essentials to good communication and listening skills.

- Listening is a very important part of communication and it is valuable to think about the purpose of your conversation with a teen.
- By removing your "fixer hat" in conversations with teens, your well-intentioned "righting-reflex" can be tamed. It then becomes easier for you to listen with empathy and the intent to understand a teen's perspective.

- Avoiding roadblocks to listening can be extremely helpful in both bettering your communication with a teen and improving your relationship with them.

- A summary is a conversational tool which involves you collecting what the teen has said and offering it back to them. Using summaries in conversations helps you to show the teen that you really are trying to understand their point of view.

DODGE IT!	TRY IT!
Roadblocks to listening.	Wearing your listening hat.
	Helpful steps for enhancing your listening skills.
	Summarize what the teen has said.

Chapter 5

MOTIVATION

I would like to invite you to take a few minutes and reflect on the questions below.

- What does it mean to "motivate teens"?
- What does it mean to "increase teens' inner motivation" for change?
- What is the difference between the two?

Thinking back to some of your previous conversations with teens, have you attempted to "motivate them" or "increase their inner motivation" for change?

There is a vast difference between *motivating* someone to change and *increasing a person's inner motivation* for change. I illustrate this difference using the two pictures below.

Some examples of things that adult helpers might like to motivate teens to accomplish are presented below and can be written in the box in the picture on the left.

1. Get up for school
2. Get better grades
3. Stop drinking, smoking, or doing drugs
4. Hang out with different friends
5. Engage in an extracurricular activity

In my Motivational Interviewing (MI) training sessions, participants often wonder how to motivate teens to, among other things, accomplish the examples in that list. My answer is simple. They don't and shouldn't. When communicating using MI, it is **not** our role as adult helpers to *motivate* a teen to do something because this implies that motivation is something that can be *instilled* in them (Miller & Rollnick, 2013). Motivation is not something that can be scooped up with a spoon and fed to someone! No matter how hard we try, it is very difficult (I would even say impossible) to *motivate* anyone, let alone a teenager, to do something that they do not want to do. Teens need to think and feel that they can, have good reason to, need to, are prepared to, or are willing to make a change.

Using MI involves having a conversation with a teen about why and how they might change the way they do things. When expressed verbally, this "motivational language", or what MI people call *change talk*, is what we listen for, explore, and evoke more of to influence motivation (Miller & Rollnick, 2013). Listening for, recognizing, exploring, and evoking a teen's change talk is central to increasing their inner motivation for change and is the "heart set" of MI (Miller & Rollnick, 2013).

Noticing change talk in any conversation depends on the conversational context in which it is heard. Change talk and it's opposite (known to MI people as "sustain talk") is highly connected to the discussion topic or focus of the conversation (Miller & Rollnick, 2013). This means that a particular statement can be a change talk statement in one context, a sustain talk statement in another context, or neither in a third context. Consider the same statement below in different conversational contexts.

Conversational Context or Focus	Statement	Statement type
Cheating on a test	*"No way! I'm not going to do that!"*	Change Talk
Confide in an adult when something is bothering them	*"No way! I'm not going to do that!"*	Not Change Talk (Sustain Talk)
Not wanting to be told what to do, for example coming home in time for curfew	*"No way! I'm not going to do that!"*	Neither Change Talk nor Sustain Talk

Quiz: Identifying Change Talk

Objective: To identify which statements are change talk statements.

Instructions: The quiz includes a teen's verbal statements, that can either be change talk statements or not. Can you tell the difference?

1. Conversational context or focus: Take care of the family pet.

   "I'll take the dog for a walk when I get home from school."

2. Conversational context or focus: School work.

   "I hope I get a better grade on this test."

3. Conversational context or focus: Make it to school on time.

   "I might make it to school on time if I went to bed earlier."

4. Conversational context or focus: Handle feelings of depression.

   "I cannot keep feeling like this. I need to talk to someone who can help me."

5. Conversational context or focus: Improve a relationship with a parent.

   "I am prepared to try."

6. Conversational context or focus: Get a job.

   "Yesterday, I went to three places about a summer job."

7. Conversational context or focus: Quit smoking.

   "I love smoking. It makes me look cool."

8. Conversational context or focus: Do school work.

   "I just need to accept that I am stupid. That's just the way it is."

9. Conversational context or focus: Do school work.

   "I would way rather be with my friends than doing school work."

10. Conversational context or focus: Handle a situation without violence.

    "If I beat her up, then I will probably get suspended or something."

11. Conversational context or focus: Handle a situation without violence.

    "Someone has to teach him a lesson!"

12. Conversational context or focus: Refrain from drinking at a party.

    "Absolutely not! Are you crazy?"

For answers, please see the key on pages 195-196.

Self-reflection

- What was your experience from the quiz?
- What did it encourage you to think about?

In conversations, change talk statements can be mixed in with other types of statements (neutral statements or statements against change/ sustain talk). It can be very helpful to tune your ears to recognize and pick out the change talk, almost like recognizing the flowers in a field of weeds (Miller & Rollnick, 2013).

Quiz: Recognizing the Change Talk

Objective: To practice recognizing change talk intertwined within conversations.

Instructions: The quiz includes a teen's verbal statements including some change talk. Can you recognize and pick out the change talk?

1. Conversational context or focus: Help with chores.

   "I'm sorry. I'd like to help you with the laundry, but I just don't have the time."

2. Conversational context or focus: Continue engaging in a sport.

   "I used to like going to basketball practice but it's just not fun anymore."

3. Conversational context or focus: Working out a conflict.

   "Janet is my best friend, but she just isn't treating me very nicely. I guess I should talk to her about it."

4. Conversational context or focus: Quit smoking.

   "It's pretty expensive to smoke but there are always ways to bum cigarettes off people."

5. Conversational context or focus: Handle anxiety.

   "I suppose it might help to talk to a counsellor about my anxiety but I'm not sure that I am ready."

6. Conversational context or focus: Refrain from drinking alcohol.

   "Everybody was drinking at the party this weekend and I had to be the driver. I wish I could've had fun too. But, it was so annoying watching everyone stumble around and slur their words."

7. Conversational context or focus: Asking an older sibling to buy alcohol.

   "My older brother is so annoying. I know I shouldn't have asked him to buy me booze but he could've at least done it just this once."

For answers, please see the key on page 197.

Self-reflection

- What was your experience from the quiz?
- What did the quiz encourage you to think about?
- In your next conversation with a teen, how important is it to you to recognize their change talk, on a scale from 0-10, where 0 means *not at all important* and 10 means *very important?*

A Teen's Motivation

Think back to the reflection questions at the beginning of this chapter and to the difference between *motivating* a teen to change and *increasing a teen's inner motivation* for change.

I invite you now to think of your role as helping teens discover what they are already motivated to do or discover their inner motivation for change, as illustrated by the question marks in the picture on the left. The question marks represent the things that drive or motivate a teen forward and closer to reaching their goals. However, be mindful that a teen's motivation (question marks) may not be the "something" that we *think* they should be motivated by.

Getting to know a teen and learning how they "tick" is essential to establishing an environment in which change may take place (see Chapter 3). As a helping adult, getting to know and figuring out what motivates a particular teen is an important first step, and your job is to harness whatever excites and drives that individual to encourage change. For example, a teen may be motivated to cut down their drinking to reduce their parent's "nagging," not because they think they have a problem with alcohol. MI assumes that all people are more (or less) motivated by or towards something. What is important to remember here is that not everyone is motivated by the same things or to the same extent. The degree of motivation we feel to do something depends on how *willing*, *ready*, and *able* we are.

 One way of finding out what motivates teens (to describe the question marks), is to discuss a teen's values and what is important to them. Exploring and discussing values with teens was presented in more detail in Chapter 3.

Understanding Motivation

Motivation can be defined as the driving forces, internal or external, behind a teen's actions. Put simply, motivation is the reason why teens do what they do. A teen may be motivated to receive an external reward (i.e., higher allowance, new clothes, better grades, or social status) or to avoid punishment. This type of motivation is called *external* or *extrinsic* as the driving force comes from outside the teen. A teen is *internally* or *intrinsically* motivated when the driving force comes from within them. Intrinsic motivation occurs when teens do things for their own sake and for their own reasons, and because engaging in that particular action is important to them. As shown in the illustration above, intrinsic motivation is represented by the question marks on the teen's shirt.

Motivation then is not considered to be a static characteristic or attribute that a teen either has or doesn't have. Instead, motivation is seen as something which can be influenced through conversation. A teen's motivation can be affected by their environment (i.e., school and home) and by the people around them (i.e., their friends and family).

Our Basic Psychological Needs

Motivation is what moves people to action. According to Self-Determination Theory (SDT), humans have three basic psychological needs that naturally draw us towards growth, development, and well-being

(Deci & Ryan 1985, 2012; Ryan & Deci 2018). These three basic psychological needs – competence, relatedness, and autonomy – interact with and affect each other.

SDT focuses on how satisfaction of these basic psychological needs increases our intrinsic (inner) motivation and influences our choices and behaviour. When these three needs are not satisfied, an individual will become frustrated and may show this frustration by becoming defiant or passive. However, when these three needs are satisfied, an individual can flourish thereby facilitating vitality, motivation, social integration, and well-being (Deci & Ryan 1985, 2012; Ryan & Deci 2018).

The satisfaction of these basic and natural psychological needs is highly dependent on an individual's social and environmental context. In other words, it is important to provide the necessary environments designed to support and satisfy these psychological needs for all individuals. Ryan & Deci (2018) describe the need for competence, relatedness, and autonomy, and their supportive environments as follows.

- **COMPETENCE** – The need for *competence* refers to our basic need to be confident in our own ability to cope with, and succeed in, what we do. We need to feel capable in our ability to master tasks or situations within our social environments. An environment that supports an individual's competence is one including positive feedback and encouragement, consistency, and structure.

- **RELATEDNESS** – The need for *relatedness* refers to feeling socially connected to others. We need to be a part of and belong to a social community to feel loved and valued in a social context. Relatedness also refers to experiencing oneself as giving or contributing to others, being significant and mattering to others (Ryan & Deci, 2018). A supportive environment is one involving others who care and where an individual is given the opportunity to both give to, and receive from, those around them.

- **AUTONOMY** – We need to feel free to choose and decide the path ahead and be in control of our own lives. Ryan & Deci (2018) explain the need for *autonomy* as the basic need to self-regulate one's own experiences and actions. These actions are ones we do because we want to do them, and they are in agreement with our inherent interests and values. Ryan & Deci (2018) define autonomous actions as behaviours engaged in "wholeheartedly" (pg. 10). For example, if we are not allowed to make our own choices or decisions, or we are forced to do something we do not want to do, our need for autonomy is unsatisfied. An environment that supports the basic need for autonomy is one offering choices and encouraging self-regulation, instead of an over-controlling or demanding environment.

Exploring Motivation

Exploring motivation entails helping teens voice their own arguments for change, evoking, or calling forth their change talk (Miller & Rollnick, 2013). Now, take a moment and think about something you might want to change in your own life. For example, you might want to get more exercise or to eat more fruits and veggies, to improve your communication with a teen, to be more patient with a teen, or to better understand a teen's point of view. Now reflect on how motivated you feel when you *think* about it, if you were to *say* it out loud *to yourself*, or if you were to *say* it out loud *to someone else*. The idea behind this is that people will talk themselves into change and become more committed to doing what they hear themselves say out loud (Miller & Rollnick, 2013).

Exploring a teen's motivation involves helping a teen to express their own motivations and reasons for change. We want to evoke a teen's change talk so that she/he can hear it, recognize it, and act on it.

Rulers as Conversational Tools

There are different ways you can explore motivation and evoke change talk. One way is by simply asking open-ended questions (Miller & Rollnick, 2013), such as:

- What are your reasons for wanting to _____?
- What ideas do you have for how you *could* change?
- How do you want your life to be a year from now?
- How serious or urgent does this feel to you?

Another way to explore motivation and evoke change talk is by using rulers, or scales, in conversations with teens. These rulers guide you when exploring a teen's willingness, readiness, and ability to do something.

Willingness/Importance

How important is it for you to _____ on a scale from 0 – 10, where 0 means *not at all important* and 10 means *very important?*

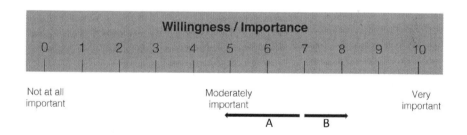

A. What makes it so important to you that you rate it as a____ for importance and not a____ (lower number)? (evoke change talk)

B. What do you think would need to happen to increase your number to a____ (higher number)? (evoke change talk)

Ability/Confidence

How confident are you that you *can* _____ on a scale from 0 – 10, where 0 means *not at all confident* and 10 means *very confident*?

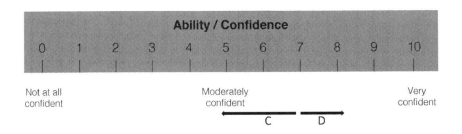

C. What makes it at a _____ for confidence and not a _____ (lower number)? (evoke change talk)

D. What do you think is needed for you to increase your number to a ___ (higher number)? (evoke change talk)

Readiness

How *ready* are you to_____, from 0 – 10?

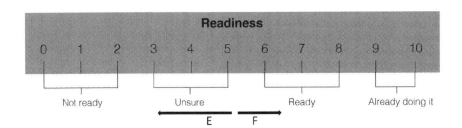

E. What makes you rate your readiness as a___ and not a___ (lower level)? (evoke change talk)

F. What do you think is needed for you to increase your readiness to a___ (higher level)? (evokes change talk)

What do you notice about these questions? The rulers/scales are used to evoke the reasons for change, not the reasons NOT to change. When we are attempting to increase a teen's inner motivation for change, we stay away from evoking the negative reasons for change, for example why a teen would not want to, why they are unable to and why they are not ready to change.

Take a moment to reflect what would happen if you were to ask a teen, *"what are your reasons for rating a 6 and NOT a 10?"* The teen might answer, *"because I don't have the time"* or *"I have better things to do"* or *"I can't"*. That's right! We have mistakenly evoked the teen's reasons NOT to change and now we are encouraging them to talk themselves OUT of change. Remember that people become more committed to doing what they hear themselves say out loud (Miller & Rollnick, 2013).

HELPFUL TIPS

It can be extremely helpful to encourage exploration and listen to the teen with empathy, for example using summaries. Regard the teen's arguments and reasons for changing with non-judgement and acceptance. Note that it is not always the easiest task when our "righting-reflex" is triggered and our "fixer hat" is cemented onto our head.

HELPFUL TIPS

Let your creativity soar. The ruler as a conversational tool uses numbers as a way of engaging a teen in conversation about change. The most important thing is the motivational language (change talk) stemming from the use of the tool, not the tool itself. Getting creative and by thinking outside of the box, you could use illustrative pictures (face emojis or a seedling becoming a tree) for example.

Exercise: Exploring a Teen's Change Talk

Objective: To explore a teen's motivation for change by evoking change talk.

Instructions: Conduct a conversation with a teen about their inner motivation and reasons for change using the three rulers. Examples of conversation topics could be:

- Get up for school
- Get better grades
- Stop drinking, smoking, or doing drugs
- Hang out with different friends
- Engage in an extracurricular activity
- Coming home on time (abiding by your curfew)
- Having a better attitude

Self-reflection

- How do you feel the conversation went?
- What new things did you learn about the teen?
- What important things did you hear the teen say?
- How can you incorporate this in your everyday interactions with the teen?

You can use all three of these rulers together in the same conversation or you can use them one at a time, in separate conversations. It depends on you, the teen, and the subject. For example, say that you and a teen have agreed that the teen will do an extra 30 minutes of school work every day. You might decide on the readiness scale to test the waters and ask, *"How ready are you to do an extra 30 minutes of school work every day, from 0 – 10?"* This way you will get some quick information as to where the teen is immediately after your conversation.

Chapter Wrap-Up

This chapter discussed understanding and exploring a teen's motivation for change.

- Getting to know a teen and learning how they "tick" is essential to establishing an environment for which change can take place.
- The best motivation comes from within and is not a static attribute which can be instilled in someone.
- There is a difference between *motivating* a teen to change and *increasing* a teen's *inner motivation* for change.
- Recognizing and exploring a teen's own reasons for change (known as "change talk") and helping them express those reasons out loud is essential when attempting to increase their inner motivation for change.
- Rulers, or scales, can be used to explore motivation and evoke a teen's change talk.

DODGE IT!	TRY IT!
Trying to install or instill motivation.	Increasing a teen's *inner* motivation for change.
	Explore a teen's motivation using rulers.

Chapter 6

ELICITING MOTIVATION

otivational interviewing (MI) is a collaborative conversational style and a way of interacting with other people. The mindset, or *spirit*, consists of the following basic principles (Miller & Rollnick, 2013):

- Establishing a collaborative relationship and becoming a "team" with the other person.
- Showing genuine compassion for the needs of the other person.
- Seeing and believing in another's strengths and positive resources.
- Being non-judgmental towards another person and of their thoughts, feelings, and perspectives.
- Respecting and understanding another's basic need to make their own choices.

The cornerstones of MI are described in more detail below and the exercises provided invite you to practice MI in your daily conversations with teens.

Active Collaboration (Partnership)

Establishing a collaborative relationship, and encouraging "team spirit," is about communicating with a teen from their point of view. An active collaboration involves viewing the teen as their own person with knowledge, experience and ideas that can complement your own knowledge, experiences, and ideas. This means that even though you are an adult, you are not the only expert in the relationship.

HELPFUL TIPS   Be mindful not to wear your "expert hat."

Have you ever found yourself in a "wrestling match" with a teen in your circle? If you have, you are not alone. This morning, I ended up in a wrestling match with my daughter. She was very tired and did not want to get out of bed when the alarm went off. I nagged and pestered her. She became more and more irritated with me, and me with her. However, my nagging and pestering did not make any difference. Despite all my "reminders," I still had to jump in the car, wearing only my robe, with my wet hair in a towel and quickly drive her to school. It was not a good start to my day. We did not collaborate, and we definitely did not win any medals for working as a functioning team.

Instead of a wrestling match where both parties are focused on "winning," an active collaboration (partnership) should feel more like a ballroom dance, where both parties work together to reach their goal (Miller & Rollnick, 2013). This morning, I do not think my daughter and I shared the same goal, which was that she should get to school on time in a calm and timely manner. So, what could I have done differently?

When my daughter came home from school that day, we talked about the morning's drama. This was our conversation.

Me: *How do you think things went this morning?* (Explore)

Daughter: *Not so good. I didn't want to get out of bed this morning. I was really tired, and you are always so happy in the mornings…and I'm not.*

Me: *We function differently in the mornings, you and I. And some days it is harder to get out of bed. What do you think makes it stressful for you in the mornings?* (reflect her words, exploring more)

Daughter: *It is stressful…..yes mom I knowwwwwww….I'm sorry… I knoooooowwwwww.*

Me: *So, you've also thought about what happened this morning. Can I tell you what it is like for me when this happens in the mornings?* (asking permission to share my thoughts)

Daughter: *Yes but I knnoooooooowwww Moooommmmm.*

Me: *Hmmm…I think you might actually know. Tell me what you're thinking then. How do you think these mornings affect me?* (affirm her, explore her ideas)

Daughter: *You feel stressed out and might be late for work if you have to drive me.*

Me: *You got it. I do feel stressed, just like you feel stressed about being late for school. In that sense, we share the same feeling. There is one more thing that I would like to share with you…may I?* (validate her thoughts, ask permission to share how I feel)

Daughter: *Yes*

Me: *I don't like it when we say goodbye to each other in the middle of all that stress and irritation. That makes me feel sad and sometimes that feeling can stay with me throughout the day. What do you think when you hear me say that?* (give my perspective, explore what she thinks about my point of view

Daughter: *Me too, but I told you I loved you before I got out of the car…*

Me: *Yes…I heard that, and I told you I loved you too…..So, I'm thinking that you and I kinda think the same here. Neither one of us like feeling stressed in the mornings or those other feelings we have when we say goodbye. Did I get that right?* (summarize and get feedback from her)

Daughter: *Yes*

Me: *What do you think we can do to stop that from happening again?* (explore solutions)

Our conversation continued and included a discussion of solutions to make our mornings a little easier.

What do you think? Did the conversation above feel to you more like a wrestling match or a dance where we moved together, back and forth, towards a common solution?

The Conversational Tool: Explore-Offer-Explore (EOE)

The tool presented in the dialogue above is called Explore – Offer – Explore (EOE). These three steps are extremely useful when establishing an active collaboration (partnership) and help to develop and enrich the relationship between you.

Below is a description of EOE using examples from the dialogue above.

Step 1: Explore the teen's perspective first (before you offer your perspective)

> *"How do you think things went this morning?"*
> *"How do you think it affects me?"*

Step 2: Ask permission to **Offer** your view of the situation

> *"Can I tell you what it is like for me when this happens in the morning?"*
> *"There is one more thing that I would like to share with you…may I?"*

An important aspect of this step is to ensure that you **respect** the teen's right to choose *not* to hear your perspective at that precise moment. If the teen answers "no," then you can follow up with a question as to when would better suit them to discuss your perspective and try again at that time.

Once you have received permission from the teen, you may offer your perspective or view of the situation.

"I don't like it when we say goodbye to each other in the middle of all that stress and feel a little irritated with each other. That makes me feel sad and sometimes that feeling can stay with me throughout the day."

Step 3: Explore the teen's understanding of what you have shared

"What do you think about that?"

Exercise: Partnership/EOE

Objective: To practice creating a "team spirit" by testing the tool EOE.

Instructions: Think back to a conversation you have had with a teen close to you that felt more like a wrestling match than a cooperative dance. What kinds of suggestions or solutions were you itching to give in that situation? For example, tips regarding a teen's homework, curfew, smoking habits, stretching after a workout. If this topic is still relevant, consider bringing it up with the teen again using **EOE**. If you would rather practice **EOE** while broaching another subject, please feel free to do so. The important thing is that you try to hop in your "driver in training" car and try the tool out.

Follow the EOE-steps.

Step 1: E (Explore)

What do you think about......?

Step 2: O (Ask permission to **Offer** your view/perspective)

Is it OK if I share what/how I am thinking about…?

Listen carefully to the teen's answer. If yes, offer clear information in small doses. If no, respond by saying, *"You do not want to talk about this **right now**. When would it suit you to talk about it?"*

Step 3: E (Explore): *What do you think about that?*

Self-reflection

- How do you feel the conversation went?
- What new things did you learn about the teen?
- What important things did you hear the teen say?
- How can you incorporate this in your everyday interactions with the teen?

What if a teen lies?

Instinctively, you may want to confront a teen who you think may be lying to get at the truth. However, this can lead to the teen becoming defensive and potentially result in an argument, with both of you trying to prove and disprove each other. You start "wrestling" again. The teen may stand firm and not risk admitting that they were "wrong." In this way, the teen's needs for autonomy, competence, and relatedness are not satisfied, usually resulting in unproductive conversations.

It is helpful to shift your focus from wanting to get at the truth to putting on your "listening hat" and really trying to understand the teen's perspective. A teen may "lie" for different reasons.

- The teen is convinced that they are right.
- The teen is afraid of being judged.
- The teen feels a need to protect him/herself, or others.

- The teen does not feel safe enough in your relationship to tell you the truth right now.
- The teen feels threatened and scared to open up.

If you suspect that a teen is lying, here are some tips for effective communication.

- Listen with your "biggest ears" and "warmest eyes." If you suspect that a teen is lying, it may be helpful to put on your "listening hat" and use the steps to enhance your listening skills (See Chapter 4).

- Temporarily consider that the teen may have a good reason for withholding the truth, because of this be curious about what that reason may be.
- Be present when the teen is ready to open up.
- Support the teen's autonomy so that the teen can influence when they would be willing to talk. For example, you could say:

  "It seems that right now you feel the need to protect yourself or someone else. I am here and ready to listen when you're ready to talk."

Active Collaboration Wrap-up

As an adult, you have a lot to actively contribute to the collaborative relationship (i.e., your knowledge and experience) and at the same time, the teen also has a lot of wisdom, answers, ideas, and expertise to contribute to this relationship. A collaborative relationship means that you are partnering with the teen and working together. Your focus is establishing a shared relationship between you, dancing together on the dance floor.

DODGE IT!	TRY IT!
A wrestling match.	Building "team spirit."
Take off your "expert hat."	Use the tool Explore – Offer – Explore (EOE)

Compassion

The word "compassion" stems from the Latin word "*compati*" which means "to suffer with" (Gilbert, 2013, pg. 3). Showing compassion for another person involves being present during their struggle, as well as feeling motivated to help alleviate their pain. Compassion is showing kindness and respect for another person's needs and putting another person's needs ahead of your own (Miller & Rollnick, 2013; Gilbert, 2013).

In an emotionally charged situation with teens, our willingness and need to help can sometimes be overshadowed by our "righting-reflex" and us putting on our "fixer hat" (See Chapter 4). Even if we feel compassion and want to take care of the teen, we may also feel the need to protect ourselves from suffering or worry. The focus of a conversation can easily shift from what the teen needs in a particular moment (i.e., to be listened to with acceptance, empathy and objectivity) to what we need instead (i.e., to get rid of the difficult feelings that the conversation or situation awakened).

If you and the teen are experiencing difficulties, or if the teen is going through a rough time, it can be difficult for you to stand by and watch. As a result of this, it may be hard for you to focus on what the teen needs from you (have a *teen focus*). What all teens need most in difficult situations are compassionate, reliable, and stable adults who are brave enough to stand beside them in their suffering. To be able to do that successfully, adults are responsible for effectively taking care of their own emotional reactions. You can read more about the importance of self-care in Part Three.

Compassion Wrap-up

Compassion involves actively and consciously putting a teen's needs before your own in a conversation or situation at a point in time. Emotionally charged situations can be difficult for both you and the teen to handle. In these situations, what the teen needs most of all is an accepting and reliable adult who is capable of standing firm even during rocky times. In a situation like this, it can be extremely helpful to focus solely on the teen and take care of your own feelings and needs later.

DODGE IT!	TRY IT!
A "me" focus.	A "teen" focus.
Park your own feelings and reactions for the moment.	Focus on the teen's needs in the moment.

Wells of Wisdom

When frustrated or worried about a teen, it can be easy to focus on the negatives - what the teen does not do, cannot do, or does not possess. However, focusing on the negatives makes it harder for the teen and for you to find the motivation to make changes. MI assumes that a teen possesses the wisdom, experience, and internal strengths already within them to make changes (Miller & Rollnick, 2013). MI suggests that you see a teen and their situation through "positive eye-glasses." MI promotes recognizing what a teen is capable of, has within themselves, or already does successfully. The idea is that by focusing on the positive, the negative is automatically reduced.

Consider the following example. A teen has difficulty getting out of bed and getting to school on time. It is easier to notice, and focus on, the teen's inabilities and failures, which may result in making comments such as:

"You were late for school again!"
"How hard can it be to just get out of bed in time?"

"Maybe if you went to bed earlier, it would be easier for you to get up!"

These examples are statements that demonstrate a "negative focus".

A positive focus, in this example, would mean exploring the teen's thoughts, ideas, and suggestions around what would help them get up in the morning and get to school on time.

> *"What do you think could help you get up in the morning?"*
>
> *"What has previously helped you get up in the morning?"*
>
> *"What would you want/be willing to try?"*

A positive focus could include dropping a bucket down the teens "well of wisdom" to identify, understand, and focus on the times when the teen was **successful** in getting up and making it to school on time. This could be explored by asking some of the following questions:

> *"The last time you got up and made it to school on time, what helped you?"*
>
> *"What thoughts helped you to get out of bed?"*
>
> *"What tools or resources helped you be successful?"*
>
> *"How can you do more of this to be successful again?"*

By showing interest, and asking similar questions to the ones above, you show the teen that you "believe" that they have the solutions and answers within themselves. You believe that they already know what they need to do differently. You convey that there is wisdom in the bottom of their well!

Quiz: Difference Between a Positive and Negative Focus

Objective: To reflect on the difference between a positive and negative focus.

Instructions: The quiz includes an adult's thoughts, or verbal statements, that have either a positive or negative focus. Can you tell the difference?

	Thought/Verbal statement
1	*"My son is always late for school"*
2	*"John is doing the best that he can do"*
3	*"Why does she always have to scream and fight at home?"*
4	*"She leaves her stuff everywhere all the time"*
5	*"I wonder what helped her get up for school today"*
6	*"He's not old enough to know what's best for him"*
7	*"You probably know what works best for you"*
8	*"He probably had some good reasons for doing what he did. I need to ask him about that later"*
9	*"I have to get her to understand that what she did was wrong!"*
10	*"I should maybe ask her for her view of the situation"*

For answers, please see the key on page 198.

Self-reflection

- What was your experience from the quiz? What did it make you think about?

- How important is it to you to have a more positive focus, on a scale from 0-10, where 0 means *not at all important* and 10 means *very important?*

- What could you do to become more focused on the positives?

Here are some activities that concentrate on the development of a positive focus. The first activity asks you to reflect by yourself, and the second activity involves talking with a teen.

Exercise: Having a Positive Focus

 Objective: To practice thinking with an extra positive focus.

Instructions: Think of a person or teen with whom you sometimes find it difficult to communicate. Instead of focusing on the difficulties or negative aspects, recognize and identify their strengths and positive resources. Try to think more positively about this individual.

Self-reflection

- How did it make you feel to think more positively about the person or teen? In what way was it easy or difficult?

- How can you incorporate this in your everyday interactions with them?

Exercise: Communicating using a Positive Focus

Objective: To practice having a conversation with a more positive focus while interacting with a teen.

Instructions: Conduct a conversation with a teen about their inner strengths and positive resources. Feel free to use the following questions to aid your conversation.

- What are you most proud of?
- What works best for you right now? What makes it work well?
- What do you think makes you a good friend?
- What strengths or positive resources do you have that you can take advantage of?
- What do you think you could do about your situation?
- What positive qualities do you have?
- When have you been successful in the past?
- Which people are there for you?
- What difficulties have you dealt with in the past? How did you deal with them?

Self-reflection

- How do you feel the conversation went?
- What new things did you learn about the teen?
- What important things did you hear the teen say?
- How can you incorporate this in your everyday interactions with the teen?

Wells of Wisdom Wrap-up

In situations where very little feels positive, it is extremely important for both you and the teen to put on your "positive eye-glasses" and focus more on the positive things in a situation. It is also important for you to convey it in a way that is obvious to the teen that you do genuinely believe they have the strengths within them. Demonstrating a positive focus towards the teen or the present situation does not mean ignoring the negatives or what needs to change. It simply means that you can see the whole picture and actively choose to illuminate, and build on, what is positive and already functioning for the teen or the situation.

DODGE IT!	TRY IT!
A "negative" focus.	A "positive" focus.

Acceptance

Acceptance means being non-judgmental of another person and their thoughts, feelings, and behaviour. It involves meeting another person at their level, on their playing field. Acceptance does not mean condoning or necessarily agreeing with another's behaviour or opinions.

When it comes to teens, being non-judgmental and accepting includes the following:

- Seeing teens as they are, as distinct individuals with great value and potential.

- Respecting and honouring a teen's desire to make their own choices and decisions.
- Empathizing with a teen and understanding that there are several ways of looking at things.
- Showing a genuine interest in, and understanding of, a teen's point of view.
- Noticing, focusing on, and highlighting a teen's strengths and efforts.

A Teen's Autonomy

As discussed previously, one of a person's basic psychological needs is to feel in control and be able to influence or regulate what is happening in their own life. In this respect, teenagers are no different from the rest of us. Teens usually want to be independent individuals and make their own choices and decisions to influence their own perceived situation. This need for independence is normal, and essential for teens as they develop into adults (Hwang & Nilsson, 2011). Therefore, it is important for adults to support teens in their developmental journey towards autonomous adults, and refrain from interfering or inhibiting this development.

It is important to support a teen's autonomy for several reasons, these are to:

- Reduce a teen's impression that adults around them make decisions about them without including them.
- Increase a teen's sense of control and the ability to influence what happens in their life.
- Reduce conflicts and a teen's defensiveness so they feel understood and listened to (Ortiz & Skoglund, 2017).
- Increase your "team spirit" so that the teen talks more openly.
- Strengthen a teen by allowing them to reflect on or decide what is best for them.
- Show understanding for a teen's perspective and point of view.

Exercise: Autonomy[1]

Objective: To get acquainted with the concept of "autonomy" and demonstrate how easy it can be to undermine a teen's autonomy.

Instructions: Reflect on the following examples and determine if the teen's autonomy might be promoted or undermined.

Example 1: A soccer coach notices that one of the players could be playing differently in the game. After the game, the coach seizes the opportunity to help and gives the player the tips to improve their game. The player "listens" passively and becomes quieter throughout the conversation until they answer, *"Uh...okay coach."*

- What thoughts do you get when reading this example? What could the coach have done differently?

In this example, the coach is wearing his "expert hat" and fails to support the player's autonomy. The player would most likely benefit from the coach's tips. However, the way the tips are given is crucial for acceptance by the player.

For example, had the coach first asked an open question such as, *"How did you think your game went today?"* and listened carefully to the player's response first BEFORE giving the tips, the player's autonomy would have been supported and strengthened.

Example 2: A teen is getting help with their homework. The teen finds it very difficult and does not really understand the task. The person helping takes over and suggests what to do and how to think. The teen "listens" passively, at the same time as they become quieter and more distant.

---

[1] A special thanks goes out to Stephen Rollnick, Sebastian Kaplan and Richard Rutschman for the inspiration for this exercise (Rollnick, Kaplan & Rutschman, 2016).

What thoughts do you get when reading this example? What could the "helper" have done differently?

The fact that the teen has become quiet, and passive are signs they have stopped listening to or taking in what the "helper" is saying. The teen probably just wants to get out of there.

The "helper" could have asked open-ended questions to kick-start the teen's own thought processes. For example:

> *"Where would you look to find information about this?"*
>
> *"Can you tell me how the teacher explained it in class so maybe I could follow along?"*
>
> *"How do you learn best? By hearing it explained again, watching an explanatory video on YouTube, or reading about it?"*

Once again, the "helper" wore their "expert hat" and undermined the teen's own sense of autonomy. Supporting autonomy by asking questions is a great way to encourage teens to learn.

Example 3: A 12-year-old girl has already agreed to hang out with a friend on Friday night. Another friend calls on Friday afternoon and wants to hang out in the evening. The 12-year-old tells her mother this and that she intends to cancel her commitment to the first friend because she would rather hang out with the second friend. Automatically, the mother says, *"No! You can't do that (cancel). You've already committed to hanging with the first person. You can invite the second friend over too and all hang out together."* The 12-year-old shouts angrily, *"You don't understand anything!"* and storms away.

- What thoughts do you get when reading this example? What could the mother have done differently?

The 12-year-old daughter in this example was not given the opportunity to take responsibility for her choice because the mother made the decision for her. What could the mother have done instead?

The mother could have shown more interest in her daughter's perspective, stopped, and listened to her daughter's reasoning. Following that, the mother and daughter could together have brainstormed solutions to the daughter's dilemma, as well as discussed, the pros and cons of each alternative. This would help the daughter make a more well-informed decision, as well as encouraged the daughter to take responsibility for her decision AND for any consequences both positive and less positive.

All the previous examples demonstrate how easily an adult's actions can affect a teen's sense of responsibility and autonomy. Unintentionally, the teen has missed out on an opportunity to think for themselves. The teen is not given the opportunity to come to a decision themselves because the adults "righting-reflex" interfered. As previously mentioned, wanting the best for a teen does not always mean knowing what is best.

Self-reflection

- What are your thoughts about this exercise?
- What promotes or undermines autonomy in your way of communicating with a teen?
- How important is it to you to be more supportive in promoting a teen's autonomy, on a scale from 0-10 where 0 means *not at all important* and 10 means *very important*?
- What are your reasons for wanting to be more supportive in promoting a teen's autonomy?

Exercise: Sense of Autonomy[2]

 Objective: To further understand the concept of "autonomy" and reflect on how small variations in language can make considerable differences in a teen's sense of autonomy.

[2] A special thanks goes out to Stephen Rollnick, Sebastian Kaplan and Richard Rutschman for this exercise (Rollnick, Kaplan & Rutschman, 2016).

Instructions: Now, imagine you are a teen, hearing an adult express the following statements. Reflect on how each statement affects you.

1. "I would like to talk to you about something."
2. "I would like to talk to you about something and see what you think about it."
3. "I would like to talk to you about something and hear what you think about it. Would that be OK with you?"
4. "I've been thinking about something that happened and would really like to understand your point of view. When can we talk about it?"

Self-reflection

- How strong would you say the teen's sense of autonomy is in each statement?
- To what extent has the adult supported the teen's autonomy?

When each statement is read individually, it sounds "normal" or "ordinary," but it can affect how a teen experiences the conversation and their reaction.

Statement 1 and 2 do not give the teen much of a say as to if, and when, the conversation is going to take place. Statement 3 and 4 are expressed using language that supports a teen's autonomy.

How? In statement number 3, the adult has asked for the teen's permission to talk about "it." In statement number 4, the teen is invited to pick the time for the conversation.

In summary, small adjustments in the language have an important impact when supporting a teen's autonomy. Supporting a teen's autonomy demonstrates acceptance and empathy for the teen's feelings, thoughts, and perspective.

How to Promote and Support Autonomy in your Daily Interactions with a Teen

A teen's autonomy is promoted when you use verbal language, tone of voice, and body language that genuinely conveys that you want them to be able to make their own informed choices and decisions. In situations where there is no immediate danger to them or others in their vicinity, the aim of your interactions with teens should be to support and promote their autonomy. Some examples of verbal statements that convey "I want to trust your judgement here" and support autonomy are (Rollnick, Kaplan & Rutschman, 2016):

> *"You'll be a good judge of what's best for you."*
>
> *"It's up to you."*
>
> *"It's your choice."*
>
> *"You call the shots."*
>
> *"You know yourself best."*

Asking Permission as a Conversational Tool

Asking permission is a very good way to support and promote a teen's sense of autonomy. Asking permission involves asking a closed-ended question that the teen either answers *yes* or *no* to. Examples of questions used to support autonomy are:

> *"There is one thing that I would like to tell you about…may I?"*
>
> *"Would it work if I…"*
>
> *"Is it ok if…"*

Although an important part of it, asking permission is about more than just being polite. It is important to understand that asking permission only supports autonomy if the question is perceived by the teen as sincere and if they feel that their answer, whatever it might be, is genuinely accepted. Here an adult's tone of voice, choice of words, and body language convey whether the teen *can* give an honest answer. Sometimes a question can be "masked" as autonomy supporting but doesn't really support autonomy at all. Consider the example below.

"That's OK, isn't it?"

Reflect for a few minutes over the question, "That's OK, isn't it!?". What comes to mind?

If a teen was asked this question, would they really feel comfortable in answering honestly? Or is there a potential hidden agenda? Is there a pre-determined, concealed, or expected "right" answer? When using ask permission, it is crucial that the questions are intended to promote a teen's autonomy and are not just commands in disguise.

There are other times when we may intend to support a teen's autonomy (and ask permission) but unconsciously expect a specific answer. Here are some examples to reflect upon.

Example 1: The teen says, *"No! I have other things to do."* The invisible door to your conversation is slammed shut and the dishwasher does not get unloaded unless you do it yourself of course...

Can you relate? By asking permission like you did *("can you......?")*, you present the teen with a choice to unload the dishwasher or not. Now you have a dilemma, where you are stuck between a rock and a hard place, especially if you really wanted help unloading the dishwasher. If you were to ignore the teen's choice (*"no"*) and try to persuade them to empty the dishwasher, you are not respecting or accepting the choice they've made. This is not supporting their autonomy and will most likely lead to an Olympic sized wrestling match. Goodbye "team spirit!"

HELPFUL TIPS

Here it can be helpful to promote autonomy by saying something like, *"It is your chore/responsibility to unload the dishwasher, which is ready to be emptied. You can choose when you do it, before or after dinner. When would you like to do it?"*

Example 2: You want to talk to a teen about the consequences of smoking and attempt to promote autonomy by saying, *"Is it okay if we talk about the consequences of smoking?"* The teen answers *"no!"* The invisible conversation door has again been slammed shut, even though you may really have wanted to talk to the teen about the consequences related to smoking.

 Example 2 is about an issue that you may deem really important to discuss with the teen. One way to do this, while supporting autonomy, would be to allow the teen to choose *when* they would be willing to discuss the consequences of smoking. Some examples of how to phrase that are:

> *"I have some thoughts about the effects of smoking. When do you think we could talk about them? Now or _____?"*

> *"When would you be open to hearing some of our suggestions? Now or _____?"*

> *"When would you be open to hear some of my ideas? Now or _____?"*

Supporting a teen's autonomy by asking permission can sometimes feel uncomfortable or difficult and our "righting-reflex" can take over. We might become impatient waiting for an answer, and simply ignore the teen's choice (i.e., a *no* answer) by continuing to lecture a teen who stopped listening long ago. We might put on our "fixer hat" and focus on solving the problem (i.e., *"We could go to the pharmacy and pick up some nicotine gum to help you quit"*).

Acceptance and Autonomy

As an adult, it can sometimes feel uncomfortable to support a teen's sense of autonomy and thereby it is then difficult to promote a teen's autonomy during conversations with them. However, autonomy is a basic psychological need of all humans, and an integral part of normal adolescent development. When promoting autonomy, it is important that the teen perceives it as such (in our language, tone of voice and choice of words). One tool that can be used to promote autonomy is to ask permission. Asking permission requires you to be prepared for, and respect a teen's answer, no matter what that answer is. If this feels too difficult or uncomfortable right now, then you may want to refrain from asking permission at the moment. Don't worry! Additional conversational tools to help you support a teen's autonomy will be presented.

EOE as a Conversational Tool

I am originally from Canada and my first language is English, therefore my teens can take extra English classes as part of the Swedish school curriculum. These extra English classes are a wonderful opportunity for my children, who will probably appreciate them in the future, but do not see their value right now. So, when I say, "in the future," I mean in the very distant future. Currently, it is hard to motivate my son to attend these extra English classes as they are on Mondays between 5:00 pm and 6:20 pm, the same time as his beloved floorball practice. For me, though, having the same discussion every week has become a little monotonous and tiresome. Here is one example of my *many* attempts to encourage my son to attend his extra English class.

Son: *Mom, do I have to go to English today. It's sooooo boring!*

Me: *Yes, of course, you have to. You know that. Do we have to have this same conversation every week?*

Son: *But Moooom, nobody thinks it's fun!*

Me: *Listen...you have to go to English. That's just the way it is and later on, you'll thank me for it when you're all grown up. Quit complaining and just go. It really doesn't help to make a fuss about it every week.*

Son: *But....whhhhyyyyyyyy?*

Me: *Because...English is good for you to know. And...because of that extra English class, you get an A in your required English class at school. You are challenged in the extra English class and your teacher does everything she can to help you find it interesting.*

Son: *Challenged ???? Interesting? Everybody sits there just wanting to diiiieeee!*

Me: *You know....you really should think about what a good opportunity this is for you. If you get a good grade in the extra English class, you can use that grade instead of a lower grade from another subject. That's good, isn't it!?*

Son: *I don't care about that...Mommm! I really don't waaaaaanna go!*

Can you see how this conversation is going around in circles? My son and I are both wrestling and are not listening to each other at all. My son is not going to get his way (to quit the extra English class) and I am not going to get my son to go there, skipping with joy and without complaints. That's just how it is and although I have accepted that, these discussions still feel frustrating and tiring. So, what could I do differently?

Here comes one of my *many* attempts at a more autonomy-supporting conversation with my son about attending his extra English class.

Son: *Mom, do I have to go to English today. It's sooooo boring!*

Me: *You're really not looking forward to English class today. Yes, Ian...you have to go today too. We have already had this conversation* (reflection).

Son: *But Moooooooommm....no one thinks it's fun! Everybody just wants to dieeeee!*

Me: *You really don't think English is fun right now.....What would a "fun" English class look like to you?* (reflection, open question - show interest in my son's perspective)

Son: *Uh...what?! I don't know Mom ......*

Me: *OK....that was really hard for you to imagine.....an English class that's "fun"....hmmm ... OK ... How about this? The last time you went to English and didn't want to "diiieeeee", what did you do in that class?* (reflection, open question – show interest in the son's perspective)

Son: *I don't know....like ... group work. At least then we don't just sit there and listen to the teacher.*

Me: *Oh...OK....so you like it better when you are more active in class and when you work with others in smaller groups.* (reflection)

Son: *Yes, if I still have to go there....*

Me: *Can I suggest something?* (asking permission)

Son: *Fine...*

Me: *Do you think you could talk to your teacher about that, maybe ask if there could be more group work during the lessons?* (closed question – make a suggestion)

Son: *Well....if I still have to go there...(pause)...I guess I'll do it today then.*

Me: *Great! How do you feel about going there today?* (open question)

Son: *Fine...Can we stop talking about it now?*

Me: *Yep (and I thought..."until next week"* ☺)

What do you think? Did the conversation above feel more like a wrestling match or a dance where we moved together, back and forth, towards a common solution?

My son then talked to his English teacher about whether they could do more group work. She listened and showed understanding and acceptance for the fact that he would rather be at floorball practice on Mondays, instead of in his extra English class. She also understood his need to be more active during the lessons and responded accordingly. By doing so, she met him with a solution that suited where he was at that moment in time. At home, this resulted in fewer discussions about attendance over the following weeks.

In the example with my son, I used EOE (Explore-Offer-Explore) and asked permission to establish an active, collaborative partnership and to promote his autonomy. Below is a description of EOE again using examples from the previous dialogue.

Step 1: Explore the teen's perspective first (before you offer your perspective)

"What would a 'fun' English class look like to you?"

"The last time you went to English and didn't want to 'diiieeeee', what did you do in that class?"

The last question aims to support my son's autonomy by exploring his own ideas, opportunities, and suggestions to make the English class more bearable. I aimed to encourage his belief that he could change how he felt about attending the English class.

Step 2: Ask permission to **Offer** your view of the situation

"Can I suggest something?"

Even though my son allowed me to share my suggestions (*"fine"*), the most important part in this step was respecting my son's right to answer *"yes"* or *"no."* This was promoting his autonomy. If my son had replied that he did not want to hear my suggestion right then, I would have asked him *when* he would be willing to listen to my suggestion.

Step 3: Explore the teen's understanding of what you have suggested

"How do you feel about going there today?"

Exercise: Supporting a Teen's Autonomy Using EOE

Objective: To try having an autonomy-supportive conversation with a teen using EOE.

Instructions: Think about a conversation that you have had with a teen close to you that felt more like a wrestling match - a conversation where the teen in question, may have wanted the freedom to choose something such as helping with household chores, cleaning their room, setting a curfew, how much time they can play video games, what they should do with their monthly allowance, and so forth. Feel free to use EOE.

Step 1: E (Explore)

"In what way(s) do you think it is important to talk about ......?"

Feel free to wear your "listening hat" and use the "Helpful steps to enhance your listening skills" presented in Chapter 4.

Step 2: O (Ask permission to **Offer** your view/perspective)

"Is it OK if I share with you why it is important for me......?"

Listen carefully to the teen's answer. If their reply is yes, go ahead and offer clear information in small doses. If their reply is no, you could respond by saying, *"You do not want to talk about this **right now**. When would it suit you to talk more about it?"*

Step 3: E (Explore): Say something like, *"You know yourself best. What do you think about what I said? What would you like to do?"*

Self-reflection

- How was your experience of the conversation? How did it make you feel?
- What new things did you learn about the teen?
- What important things did you hear the teen say?
- How can you incorporate this in your everyday interactions with the teen?

Acceptance Wrap-up

Accepting, respecting, and promoting a teen's developmental process towards independence is one of the most important jobs adults have, not just parents. Strengthening a teen's basic, and normal, psychological need for autonomy needs to be the common thread throughout discussions and conversations with teens. When promoting autonomy, it is important that the teen perceives it as such (in our language, tone of voice and choice of words). One tip to help you keep this a common thread is to occasionally take a few minutes and ask yourself – What I'm doing right now ... does it promote or undermine a teen's need for autonomy?

One tool that can be used to promote autonomy is to ask permission. Asking permission requires you to be prepared for, and respect a teen's answer, no matter what that answer is. Another tool used to promote and support autonomy is Explore-Offer-Explore (EOE).

DODGE IT!	TRY IT!
Wearing your "expert hat" and/or not listening.	Showing **acceptance** by supporting and promoting a teen's autonomy.
	Ask permission and use the tool Explore-Offer-Explore (EOE).

Chapter Wrap-Up

Motivational Interviewing (MI) is a non-judgmental way of being and communicating with people while discussing change. Key concepts focused on in this chapter were:

- The cornerstones of MI and their importance for increasing a teen's inner motivation for change.
- Active collaboration (partnership) and its significance when establishing a positive relationship with a teen.
- The meaning and use of compassion in conversations with teens. This involves actively and consciously putting a teen's needs first.
- Seeing a teen as having a "well of wisdom." This means wearing your "positive eye-glasses," genuinely believing that a teen has strengths and positive resources within them and focusing more on the positive aspects of a situation.
- Acceptance and how to be non-judgmental in your conversations with teens. Acceptance for a teen's point of view includes listening to their perspective while supporting and promoting their need for autonomy.
- Using EOE (Explore-Offer-Explore) to explore a teen's perspective, asking permission before giving your own perspective, and following up by exploring what the teen thought of your perspective.

Part Two

Delving Deeper

Chapter 7

COMMUNICATE USING EOE
(EXPLORE - OFFER – EXPLORE)

Lighthouse Conversations presents ideas to help you communicate more effectively with a teen in your circle. The relational foundation consists of a secure and collaborative partnership resulting in a strong "team spirit" between you and a teen. Developing a positive relationship occurs when you familiarize yourself with a teen's perspective and learn about the things that they are interested in and value. Enriching the relationship happens by focusing on a teen's strengths and inner resources, as well as respecting their needs at a given moment. Respecting, honouring, and promoting a teen's need for autonomy is also an important part of developing a "team spirit", as well as supporting a teen's journey from childhood into adulthood. In summary, a positive relationship based on good communication arises if you:

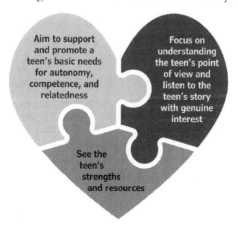

A positive relationship is extremely helpful if you would like a teen to listen to what you have to say, to understand and respect your perspective, and to make wise choices. As an adult, having a positive relationship with a teen and using effective communication skills are valuable assets if you need to:

- Say "no" and set boundaries (i.e., not allowing a teen to go to a concert or party).
- Talk about something that worries you (i.e., their social network or mental health).
- Discuss unacceptable and/or risky behaviour (i.e., skipping school, alcohol/drug use, or acts of violence).
- Inform them about something emotional or difficult (i.e., divorce or death).
- Get across some other type of important message.

To ensure that your message is effectively received it is also very important that the teen is *open* to receiving your message. This openness will hopefully encourage appropriate responses (on the teen's part) in the future, if and when necessary.

What does Openness Mean?

A teen is open to receive your message when they are ready, willing, and able to absorb, listen to, and understand what you say. The good thing is that you can influence a teen's motivation, openness, and receptivity to take in information. By encouraging the teen to be as open as possible to your message, it can help increase their motivation and willingness to do things differently in the future. The tool EOE is very good at doing just that. Using EOE increases a teen's openness and receptivity while balancing both yours and the teen's communication.

EOE can be used in many situations. It can be used in conversations with teens to give information, feedback, advice, tips, to explain something, or to deliver a message. The framework of EOE itself promotes a teen's autonomy because it focuses on the teen's perspective first before allowing you to convey your perspective. EOE also includes the tool ask permission. Let us look more closely at the three steps of EOE.

Step 1: Explore (E)

First **explore** what the teen already knows about *"what you want to say"* (This is your message). In this step, you show respect for, and interest in, the teen's thoughts, opinions, and perspectives **BEFORE** you start sharing your perspective.

Step 2: Offer (O)

Deliver, or **offer**, *"what you want to say"* (your message) in a respectful way. Step 2 begins with you first asking permission followed by expressing *"what you want to say"* (your message).

"Would it be OK if I told you what I am thinking?

"Would you care to listen to my suggestions?"

"Would you like to hear some ideas that I have?"

As previously described, the following questions can also be used to promote a teen's autonomy by allowing a teen to choose themselves *when* it would be best for them to discuss *"what you want to say"* (your message).

"I have had some thoughts about…. When do you think we could talk about them? Now or _____?

"When would you be interested in hearing some of our suggestions? Now or _____?"

"When would you be interested in hearing some of my ideas? Now or _____?"

This step helps to increase a teen's openness while respecting their autonomy. You show respect for the teen by not duplicating information they are already familiar with and by prioritizing your information based on what is most interesting to the teen.

Things to Think About in Step 2

- Deliver only messages that are relevant to the teen – what do they really NEED to know?

- If your message contains a lot of information, divide it into smaller doses and offer it visually in a menu or agenda. Allow the teen to choose the order in which they would like to hear the parts of your larger message.

Step 3: Explore (E)

Lastly, **explore** how *"what you said"* (your message) was perceived by the teen. In this step, you are interested in getting feedback about *"what you said"* (your message), or the information provided in step 2 by asking, for example:

"How did it feel to hear this?"

"What do you think about what I have shared with you?"

"What did you make of that?

Case Example: EOE

A man has been sighted in your neighbourhood, where mainly young people often hang out, offering alcohol and/or drugs to them. This information was posted by the Community Police Officer and Outreach Worker for your area on a local neighbourhood Facebook group of which you are a member. This information bothers you and is therefore extremely important to bring up with the teen in your circle.

> Adult: *Hey ... I would like to talk to you about something I saw on the local neighbourhood Facebook group. When do you have a spare minute?* (Ask permission, support autonomy)
>
> Teen: *I guess now is OK.*
>
> Adult: *Oh...great...thanks, I appreciate it. Have you heard about the man hanging around the town square trying to talk to kids and young people?* (show appreciation, closed question)
>
> Teen: *No...what do you mean?*
>
> Adult: *OK...you haven't seen this man in the square.* (reflection)
>
> Teen: *No...*
>
> Adult: *The police and outreach workers warned us about a man offering alcohol and/or drugs to young people in the area....(pause)...what are your thoughts about that?* (open-ended question)
>
> Teen: *Huh....I didn't know that. Oh God ... you're in a neighbourhood Facebook group? How embarrassing!*
>
> Adult: *Yes, I am. Lots of people post in that group, about burglaries, lost cats, and other stuff.*
>
> Teen: *Mmm ...*
>
> Adult: *So ... if you were to see this man when you're out and about with your friends, what would you do?* (open-ended question)

Teen: *If I were to see him and he started talking to me or my friends, I would tell him to "get lost" or something....I wouldn't take anything he tried to give me....if he actually was to try.*

Adult: *That is wise!! You would say no to whatever he offered and tell him to "get lost" ... Can I share with you what I would like you to do if he came up to you and started talking to you?* (affirmation, ask permission)

Teen: *OK.......*

Adult: *Thanks!.....I would really like you (and your friends too hopefully) to walk away, call one of us, and come home right away (alone or with your friends). So that we can decide together what to do about it. Maybe call the police or something.... I mean.....it depends on the situation of course. But....anyway.....the main thing is that you immediately walk away from the situation....(pause)...How does that sound to you?* (show appreciation, give suggestion, open-ended question)

Teen: *Yeah...OK....but it should just be enough to just tell him to "get lost".*

Adult: *You think this man would listen to you if you asked him to leave you alone. Well ... hopefully, that is enough, and he does. That made me think of something else. Can I share those thoughts with you too?* (reflection, ask permission)

Teen: *Yeeeesssss ... Moooommmmm.* (a little impatiently)

Adult: *We know absolutely nothing about this man. I mean, if he suffers from a mental illness or something...what you say could trigger him to become violent or something....So that's why I would like you to walk away from the situation, contact us right away, and come home ... with or without your friends. What are your thoughts about that?* (give a suggestion, open-ended question)

Teen: *Yes, OK...I get it. I didn't think about it like that.*

Chapter Wrap-Up

This chapter introduced a conversational tool called Explore-Offer-Explore (EOE) which consists of three steps.

- A positive relationship is necessary to explore and listen to a teen's point of view and affirm their strengths and resources.

- A teen's motivation, openness, and receptivity to appreciate what you have to say can be increased by using the conversational tool EOE.

- EOE includes exploring the teen's perspective, offering your message in a respectful way, and exploring how your message has resonated with the teen.

- When delivering your message, it is important to respect, honour, and promote the teen's need for autonomy.

Chapter 8

STEP 1: EXPLORE (E)

The purpose of this step is to appreciate and understand the teen's point of view by fully exploring their perspective using active listening skills. This step is essential because it:

- Conveys respect to the teen.

- Conveys compassion.

- Allows a teen to express and explore their own perspective and point of view.

- Demonstrates our intent to learn about and understand the teen's perspective.

Active listening is fundamental to good communication. It is useful to avoid misunderstandings and further assists in developing and enriching your relationship with a teen. Active listening is also one way to show empathy. Active listening includes:

- Getting and being READY to talk.

- Affirming a teen.

- Asking open-ended questions.

- Forming reflections.

READY to Talk

When preparing for a conversation with a teen, it can be helpful to set aside the time for it, generate the necessary conditions required for effective communication, and be physically and mentally present. In order words, it is extremely important for you to *get* READY for conversations with teens. It is also important for you to *be* READY when a teen invites you to communicate. This means that you need to be available and responsive when the time demands, as well as focused on understanding what the teen deems interesting and important enough to tell you about at that moment. If a teen happens to catch you at a "bad" time and you are unable to properly wear your "listening hat," you could say for example, *"Right now, I am not able to listen properly... in the way that I would like to be able to listen to you. In about 15 minutes though, I would be ready, willing, and able to listen. Does that work?"*

Respect the teen - think about how you can show respect and accept the teen and their perspectives/points of view.

Engage in the conversation – be present and involved in the current conversation. Avoid making routine statements, such as *"you've done your homework, right?"* Instead, slow down and take your time and show interest and curiosity for the teen. Feel free to put your phone down for a little while so you can fully engage in your conversation. You may learn something new.

Accept – observe and accept the teen and their reactions. What are the teen's non-verbal signals telling you? Be curious about what the teen is trying to tell you with their body language, facial expressions, and tone of voice.

Deep breaths – Ensure to calm yourself down, breathe deeply, and anchor yourself in the present. Park any previous irritations and arguments and try to cope with any powerful emotions you may have.

Your gift – be grateful and accept the teen's invitation to talk. It really is a gift!

Affirming

Exercise: Recognizing the Positives

Objective: To recognize, identify, and focus on the positives within a teen and to reflect on the concepts of affirming and praising.

Instructions: The next time a teen opens up to you about something, whatever that may be, listen attentively to the teen's story and focus on the positive, internal resources, strengths, and qualities that the teen reveals.

Self-reflection

- How was your experience of the exercise or conversation? How did it make you feel?
- Who talked the most during the conversation?
- What important things did you hear the teen say?
- What reactions in the teen did you notice?
- How can you incorporate these tips in your everyday conversations with the teen?

Affirmation Versus Praise

Example: A 14-year-old girl stands up for herself and says "no" when her friends want her to ask her older sibling to buy them alcohol for a party.

What would you like to say to her? Perhaps something along the lines of what is written below.

> *"That was good!"*
> *"Well done!"*
> *"I am so proud of you."*
> *"You are so great!"*

Have you praised or affirmed her? And does it matter which it is?

Difference Between Praise and Affirmations

Most people enjoy receiving compliments or positive comments about themselves. There is, however, a difference between praising some-one and affirming them. Praise often focuses on a person's actions or behaviour, or the result of their actions or behaviour. One situation where praise is often used between adults and children is when a child shows an adult a drawing and gets the standard, *"Ohhh … what a beau-tiful painting you've done!"*

The art of affirming is explained as an "intentional" way of commu-nicating meant "to seek and acknowledge the person's strengths and efforts" (Miller & Rollnick, 2013, pg. 19). Thus, the art of affirm-ing is much *more* than highlighting the positives (i.e., *"you are good at that"*). It means showing the teen that you *see* them for who they are and appreciate them as an individual. It also involves *seeing* the teen rather than their actions by separating the individual from their actions. It is a *conscious decision* to put on your "positive eyeglasses," as well as to highlight and put into words a teen's:

- Values.
- Good efforts and steps in the right direction.
- Strengths.
- Positive attributes.
- Good intentions and actions.
- Past successes.

Affirming has many benefits for the teen themselves, as well as for the relationship between the two of you. When you affirm a teen, you show acceptance and convey empathy, as well as show a willingness to understand a teen's perspective. Affirmations enrich the relationship between both of you, and strengthen the "team spirit," supporting the teen's need for relatedness (See Chapter 5). In turn, affirmations help a teen learn to recognize and identify the positives within themselves, enhancing their self-esteem, improving their self-image, and speaking to their need for competence (See Chapter 5).

Being Affirming

You can highlight the positives within a teen both non-verbally (i.e., with "big ears" and "warm eyes") or verbally with both general or specific affirmations (i.e., a "thank you" or an affirmative statement).

"Thank you so much for helping with the dishes."

"How nice that you came today! Here we go."

"Thanks for telling me."

"The fact that you told me was a big step."

One way to affirm a teen is using the acronym: **VASE**[3]. These positive statements are called "affirmations."

Values: What a teen deems important to help them prioritize.

Attributes: Positive characteristics and inner qualities a teen possesses.

Strengths: Strengths and resources that are within a teen or in their social network. Past successes.

Efforts: Efforts and steps taken by the teen.

 Affirmations often start with the pronoun "you," instead of "I."

---

[3] Many thanks to the Motivational Interviewing Network of Trainers (MINT) for this acronym.

Let's return to the example of the 14-year-old girl who said "no" to her friends when they wanted her to ask her older sibling to buy them alcohol. How could we affirm her using **VASE**?

Values   The girl wanted to do the right thing.

"It's important for you to do the right thing."

Attributes   Assertive, brave, determined

"Standing up for yourself really showed how assertive you are."

"You were really brave to stand up for yourself like that."

Efforts   The girl was trying to do the right thing and abide by the law.

"You are really making an effort to do the right thing."

Strengths   Strong, courageous

"You are a really strong girl who had the courage to say no."

Exercise: Helpful Affirmations Using VASE

Objective: To practice recognizing, identifying, exploring, and verbalizing a teen's **V**alues, **A**ttributes, **S**trengths, and **E**fforts (VASE).

Instructions: Listen to a teen the next time they talk about something frustrating or difficult. Try to recognize, identify, and explore one of the following: **V**alues, **A**ttributes, **S**trengths, or **E**fforts (VASE). If you want to, you can use the following questions to help guide your listening.

Values: What values or priorities can you see within the teen?

Attributes: What qualities or attributes are evident within the teen?

Strengths: What strengths do you see in the teen? What resources are evident in the teen's network?

Efforts: What effort(s) is the teen making?

Self-reflection

- How was your experience of the exercise or conversation? How did it make you feel?
- Who talked the most during the conversation?
- What important things did you hear the teen say?
- What reactions in the teen did you notice?
- How can you incorporate these tips in your everyday conversations with the teen?

Exercise: Discussing Past Successes

Objective: To familiarize yourself with and practice having a conversation about past successes.

Instructions: Conduct a conversation with a teen about a past success or a challenging situation that they handled successfully. Use the following questions if you need to.

- How did you handle the situation?
- What helpful strategies did you use to help you succeed?
- What personal attributes, characteristics, or qualities helped you handle this challenge?
- What strengths usually help you in challenging situations?

Self-reflection

- How was your experience of the exercise or conversation? How did it make you feel?
- Who talked the most during the conversation?
- What important things did you hear the teen say?
- What reactions in the teen did you notice?
- How can you incorporate these tips in your everyday conversations with the teen?

Exercise: Discussing Personal Attributes

 **Objective**: To familiarize yourself with, and practice having a conversation about, a teen's personal qualities and attributes.

Instructions: The next time a teen opens up to you about something, whatever that may be, listen attentively. Use this opportunity to explore the teen's positive characteristics, qualities, and attributes by asking open-ended questions. You may use the following questions to guide you.

- Use five adjectives to describe yourself.
- What do you think are your best qualities or attributes?
- When was the last time you used …(quality or attribute)?
- Which aspects of yourself do you like the most?
- What are you good at? What is it that makes you good at it?

 If a teen has difficulty describing him or herself, you can warm them up by exploring the qualities or attributes that they appreciate in others. Feel free to use the following questions if you need.

- Which qualities or attributes do you value in others?
- Of those qualities or attributes, which do you possess yourself?
- Of those qualities or attributes, which do you wish you possessed? What are your reasons for wishing for that?
- Can I tell you what I see in you?
- In what way(s) could these qualities or attributes help you in the future?

Self-reflection

- How was your experience of the exercise or conversation? How did it make you feel?

- Who talked the most during the conversation?
- What important things did you hear the teen say?
- What reactions in the teen did you notice?
- How can you incorporate these tips in your everyday conversations with the teen?

Exercise: Discussing Personal Attributes Using Conversational Cards (Attribute Cards)

 **Objective**: To strengthen a teen by describing and exploring their positive qualities or attributes and to reflect on how these qualities or attributes can be helpful in different contexts (i.e., at school, in conflicts, in the family, as a friend).

Instructions: Discuss a teen's positive characteristics, qualities, and attributes using the following four steps and the Attribute Cards. Download the Attribute Cards at https://en.novovia.se/bookresources.

1. **The concept of a "positive" quality or attribute**

   Start the conversation by brainstorming the concept "positive" quality. Feel free to ask some of the following questions.

   - What qualities or attributes do you consider "positive?" Less "positive?"
   - Where do we get our qualities or attributes from?
   - How do you think our qualities or attributes change over time? What do you think are the reasons that they may improve?
   - How can we improve our qualities or attributes?

2. **Summarize**

   Tie together what the teen defines as a "good quality" and offer it back to them in a summary. More information about summaries can be found in Chapter 4.

3. Discuss positive qualities or attributes using the **Attribute Cards**

Use the Attribute Cards to discuss a teen's positive qualities or attributes. You can use the cards in two different ways:

- Place the full sheets of attribute cards in front of the teen and ask them to circle the qualities or attributes they possess, or

- Cut out the Attribute Cards in advance and ask a teen to select the cards containing qualities or attributes they possess from the deck of Attribute Cards.

Choose the way that suits you and the teen best.

4. Summarize

Put on your "listening hat" and summarize all the qualities or attributes the teen has identified. Highlight and summarize the ways in which these can be helpful as described by the teen.

Self-reflection

- How was your experience of the exercise or conversation? How did it make you feel?

- Who talked the most during the conversation?

- What important things did you hear the teen say?

- What reactions in the teen did you notice?

- How can you incorporate these tips in your everyday conversations with the teen?

Affirming Wrap-up

The art of affirming involves noticing and discovering the positive within a teen. Affirming is important for your relationship, the teen's self-esteem, and the teen's need for competence. Affirming means simply showing appreciation to the teen by saying "thank you," seeing and encouraging them with your body language, and forming an affirmation by verbalizing the teen's Values, Attributes, Strengths/resources, or Efforts (VASE).

DODGE IT!	TRY IT!
A "negative" focus.	A "positive" focus. Appreciate and see the whole teen. Affirm using VASE.

Asking Questions

The opening of a conversation can be compared to the start of a chess game, the first move puts its mark on the outcome of the rest of the game. The key to encouraging a teen to "open up" is to use open-ended questions. Open-ended questions help show interest in the teen's thought processes and explores a teen's perspectives and points of view.

Before asking questions, it may be a good idea to think about the purpose of your conversation. The purpose of the conversation determines which questions you ask and how you ask them. Take a moment to reflect on whether your conversation is meant to be supportive, motivational, informative, or fulfil another purpose.

There are different types of questions: closed, open-ended, and multiple-choice.

Closed Questions

- Ask for specific information and are often answered using short responses (i.e., yes, no, good, etc).

- Often start with a verb (i.e., *"are you...?"*, *"can you...?,* *"will you...?"*, *"do you...?"*).
- Are useful when looking for a quick and direct answer.
- Are helpful when wanting to support and promote a teen's autonomy, for example when asking permission.

 Too many closed questions can cause someone to become passive within the conversation.

Examples of closed questions are provided below

> *"Was that difficult?"*
> *"Does that work for you?"*
> *"Do you smoke?"*
> *"Have you been to school today?"*
> *"Are you going to answer me?"*
> *"Did you go to bed early?"*
> *"Are you gaming?"*

Open-ended Questions

- Are like door openers in a conversation.
- Invite a teen to express their own thoughts, feelings, and desires more freely.
- Convey your interest in the teen's story.
- Begins with question words: In what way...? Which? Who? How? What? Where?

Examples of open-ended questions are below.

> *"What has worked for you before?"*
> *"What would be helpful for you right now?"*

"What would you like…?"

"What are your thoughts about…?"

"How can I help you?"

"What do you know about…?"

"In what way is this important to you?"

"In what way is this a problem for you?"

Here is something to ponder upon and consider. Have you ever used your best open-ended question and the teen still answers with a shrug of their shoulders and an *"I don't know"* response? Well, welcome to the club. You are not alone!

It can be helpful to reflect over, and even put into words, why the teen "doesn't know." A teen may be trying to say the following instead:

"I need more time to think."

"I really don't know."

"I am having a hard time expressing myself."

"I don't have the energy to explain it."

"I don't want to tell you."

Reflecting on the reasons why a teen responds with *"I don't know"* response encourages us to be more understanding and may make it easier to respond to them in the future.

Some ideas on how to respond to a teen's shoulder shrug and *"I don't know"* response while promoting their autonomy are to:

o   Form a reflection followed by a closed question, for example:

"Right now, you don't know. Is it OK for me to check in with you later?

"That question can be kind of hard to answer … is it OK if I check with you later?

○ Use a multiple-choice question to support and promote a teen's need for autonomy.

Multiple-choice Questions

If you notice that your well-thought-out open-ended questions do not lead to the desired effect that you were hoping for (i.e., the teen does not start talking freely), it can then be helpful to switch to multiple-choice questions. Multiple-choice questions start out as open-ended questions and finish off by restricting the answer to a few alternatives (Miller & Rollnick, 2013). These questions are useful in many situations, especially in ones when a teen replies with the dreaded shoulder shrug or *"I don't know"* response. Multiple-choice questions can also be helpful if the teen has difficulty in expressing what they think or feel. It may even be helpful to provide a "blank" option so the teen could come up with their own idea. Here are a few examples.

> *"What would the reasons be for you doing it? For your own sake? To avoid my nagging? Or something else?"*
>
> *"Would it be OK for me to share some thoughts as to what might be bothering you? Some teens can feel ...X... and others may feel ...Y... What might be the closest to what you are feeling?"*
>
> *"How did it feel? Was it hard, easy or something in between?"*
>
> *"Were you perhaps feeling angry, sad, or something else?"*

You can also promote a teen's autonomy and draw attention to possible choices by using multiple-choice questions.

> *"Where would you like to start? A or B?"*
>
> *"What would you like to do? A or B?"*
>
> *"What would be the most fun for you? A, B or C?"*
>
> *"When would you be willing to chat? Now or after_____?*

Hypothetical questions can also be helpful to stimulate a conversation with a teen and encourage them to reflect on a situation or behaviour.

> *"If this happened to someone you know, what do you think they might think or feel in this situation?"*
>
> *"If it was about someone else, would you think the same way?"*

The Question Word: "Why?"

Asking "why" can be interpreted in multiple ways depending on where we come from, how we were raised, our level of education, and our own life experiences. Asking "why" is often perceived as confrontational and accusatory. Teens have most likely encountered adults who have used "why" in an accusing way, conveying a message that they should have done something differently or better. If you are curious as to why a teen acted in a certain way, use one of the open-ended "question" words instead. For example, instead of *"Why did you do that?"* you could ask *"What were your reasons for doing that?"*

Exercise: Asking Questions

Objective: To practice asking questions and preparing for a conversation.

Instructions: Prepare for the conversation by creating some open-ended questions and/or multiple-choice questions that could be helpful in your everyday conversations. Feel free to pick situations based on your everyday life to make this exercise as realistic and purposeful as possible. When you are ready, engage the teen in the conversation.

Theme/everyday examples: If you need help coming up with everyday examples, consider using some of the suggestions below to help get you started.

- Emotional well-being.
- Importance of going to school.
- Sex and use of contraceptives.
- Training habits.
- Understand that study/doing homework is necessary to get results.
- Clothing style.
- Alcohol, drugs, & gambling.
- Internet safety and grooming.
- Conflicts or relationship problems with friends.
- Societal issues or other causes for worry.

Theme - What do you want to talk to a teen about?	What questions (open and/ or multiple-choice questions) could be helpful to ask during the conversation?

Self-reflection

- How do you feel the conversation went?
- What new things did you learn about the teen?
- What important things did you hear the teen say?
- How can you incorporate this in your everyday interactions with the teen?

Questions Wrap-up

There are different types of questions that encourage effective communication with teens. Open-ended questions show your interest in a teen's thoughts and perspectives, as well as encouraging a teen to talk freely about what is of interest to them and what they personally consider important. In situations where open-ended questions do not have the desired effect, or if a teen shrugs their shoulders or replies with *"I don't know,"* it can then be helpful to use multiple-choice or hypothetical questions.

DODGE IT!	TRY IT!
The "question trap" – Avoid using too many closed questions. Avoid using *"why?"*	Use questions that explore. Use open-ended, multiple-choice or hypothetical questions.

Reflections

"The most important thing in communication is hearing what isn't said."

– Peter F. Drucker

Thomas Gordon (2019) developed a model which explains the listening process in more detail (see picture on the next page). The teen is thinking of something (the dark cloud on the left side). The teen then thinks of the things that they could say (the white cloud on the left side) and then what the teen actually verbalizes (the speech bubble). Lastly, the words that the adult hears the teen say (the dark cloud on the right side) and what the adult understands (the white cloud on the right side).

Based on this model, where can listening go wrong?

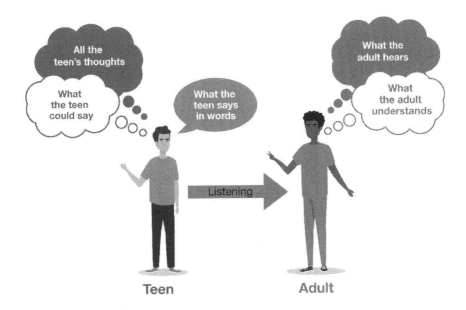

Thomas Gordon (2019) describes three common errors that can occur during listening.

- The teen does not say what they mean.
- The adult does not "hear" the teen's words correctly.
- The adult misinterprets the teen's words which consequently implies or gives them a different meaning than what was intended.

What are Reflections?

Reflections are conversational tools used to clarify information you receive from a teen and avoid the common errors in listening as described above. Reflections convey empathy because they demonstrate your active intention to understand what a teen is really trying to tell you. Miller and Moyers (2021) describe this process as "mirroring," where you attentively listen to what the teen is saying and *reflect back* your understanding of it (pg. 25). By conveying to the teen that you get them, you recognize and support their need for competence and relatedness (See Chapter 5).

Formed as statements, reflections mirror back the essence of what a teen is trying to communicate to you, using similar or different words. This does not mean *echoing* a teen's statements word for word, as that will most likely cause irritation. No one likes to be parroted! Your tone and inflection of voice here are also important. When reflecting, try and inflect your voice down at the end of the sentence (Miller, 2018).

By forming reflections, you mirror back *your* understanding (the white cloud on the right side), which is based on your interpretation or "guess" of what you heard the teen say (the dark cloud on the right side). By reflecting back what you *think* the teen means, you convey respect to the teen and allow them the opportunity to correct any misinterpretations, making sure that you and the teen are on the same page.

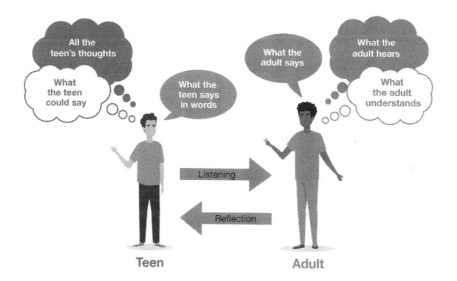

In Motivational Interviewing (MI), good reflections are formed using the word "you" to show that the teen is the only one in focus. For example, reflections can start with the following.

> "You would like to..."
> "It is important for you to...

"You are thinking that…"

"Your thoughts are…"

"You have some thoughts about…"

"Your opinion is…"

"You are sure about…"

"You wish…"

"Your experience is…"

"You are sure about…"

"You feel…"

Previously, you may have learned to show understanding for another person by using phrases such as, *"I understand that you…"* or *"I hear that you…"* or *"I see that you…."* In MI, we aim to avoid these types of statements, partly because they focus on the speaker instead of the other person, and partly because they often provoke irritation. For example, if you say, *"I understand…."* to a teen, you had better be ready to hear *"You don't understand anything."* If you have fallen into that trap, again, you are not the only one!

It may also be that the teen has previously heard an adult say, *"I understand…but"* or *"I hear that you…but."* Unfortunately, the word *but* psychologically erases everything said before it and focuses on what comes after. This use of *but* can trigger a wrestling match and lead to unintended conflict.

Consider this example. A teen in your circle suffers from depression. You would like to support them through this difficult time.

> Adult: *"I understand that everything feels dark and really difficult right now, but it will get better".*

> Teen: *"How the heck do you know it's going to get better?"*

In the example above, the adult's "need to help" took over as they started trying to persuade the teen that things will get better. An adult's subsequent response might be to say, *"This feeling shall pass because I've been there...and I know."* Although the adult was only trying to help, the focus has now shifted from the teen's experience to the adult's own experience. How do you think this switch and change will affect the teen? This is another example of how an adult wearing their "expert hat" can unintentionally hurt the collaborative relationship with a teen, as well as preventing the teen from describing the situation as they see it from their own experience.

 Instead of using an *"I understand..."* statement, an alternative answer could be a reflection, for example, *"Right now you are struggling, and it feels difficult and challenging for you."*

Exercise: Forming Reflections

Objective: To have the opportunity to practice coming up with your own reflections, read some suggestions, and learn that there can be many different responses to a situation.

Instructions: Read the examples and write down some reflections that you could say to the teen. Then read the suggestions.

Example 1: Lisa is 14 years old and has recently started cutting and harming herself on her arms. She confides that it helps her at the time, but not in the long run after the initial effect has worn off. She feels really bad about it but does not feel ready to tell you the reason she does this to make her feel better. She does not know what to do about it but doesn't want to continue like this.

Reflections:

_____

_____

_____

Suggestions

"You are struggling to find ways to manage your well-being."
"You are not feeling well right now and want to find ways to feel better."

Example 2: Anna is a 17-year-old girl who places very high demands on herself. She feels that she needs to be good at most things and has a hard time dealing with things when they go wrong. Right now, she feels bad about not knowing what to do after she finishes high school and at the same time, she is stressed about her school grades.

Reflections:

_____

_____

_____

Suggestions

"You care a lot about your future."
"You are placing high demands on yourself."

Example 3: John is 16 years old and has considered many options regarding his future career choice. Which high school stream should he pick? Which is the right one? There are so many choices that John feels unsure of what he really wants and what is the right decision. He thinks about what is best for him in the long run but also considers what his friends might choose. John has always been interested in the media but none of his friends are interested in it. Should he go along with his friends, or choose what he really wants?

Reflections:

....

....

....

Suggestions

"It is important for you to choose what matters to you."

"You want to choose carefully and think about both what is good right now and what will be best for you in the long run."

Example 4: George is a 16-year-old who is worried about the state of the world (for example climate change, covid-19). He thinks a lot about potential disasters that he believes are threateningly close. George worries a lot and has anxious experiences and thoughts that sometimes cause him to have sleepless nights. During the school day, he is also preoccupied thinking about these things and is missing important information in his school lessons.

Reflections:

....

....

....

Suggestions

"You care so much about things around you that you have a hard time concentrating."

"You really care about the world we live in."

Example 5: David is a 15-year-old who likes to play computer games. Because of this, he has many friends in the virtual world and is well known for his gaming. In the beginning, David was able to balance his gaming with other activities. However, now playing computer games has started to take over his everyday life and is having a negative effect on him. His schooling is suffering, and he is exercising less.

David is often in a bad mood and as he inverts his sleep pattern, he often loses track of time and plays late into the night.

Reflections:

_____

_____

Suggestions

"You are experiencing a change in your life now that means you are playing more and more."

"You really like playing computer games and maybe you have noticed that when you play more it seems to affect your mood."

Example 6: Ethan is 14 years old and often ends up in conflicts with his parents about his chores and responsibilities. His parents do not think he helps out enough and Ethan thinks that if his siblings did more, his parents would stop nagging him. Ethan thinks that his parents demand a lot from him as he is the oldest child.

Reflections:

_____

_____

Suggestions

"You take on the responsibilities that you feel are reasonable to you."

"It's important to you that your list of chores feels fair."

Self-reflection

- What did the exercise encourage you to think about?
- How can you incorporate this in your everyday interactions with the teen?

Exercise: Forming Reflections in a Conversation

Objective: To practice forming reflections in a conversation by mirroring back on a teen's feelings, thoughts, and experiences.

Instructions: The next time a teen opens up to you about something, whatever that may be, listen attentively. Try forming reflections to say back to the teen. The reflections may consist of the teen's feelings, thoughts, or experiences that they may or may not have expressed yet.

Self-reflection

- How was your experience of the conversation? How did it make you feel?
- Who talked the most during the conversation?
- What important things did you hear the teen say?
- What reactions in the teen did you notice?
- How can you incorporate these tips in your everyday conversations with the teen?

Reflections Wrap-up

Reflections are used to convey empathy and illustrate a willingness to understand a teen's perspective. Reflections mirror back what you think you heard the teen say, what you think the teen means and/ or what you think the teen has not yet expressed. Reflections are focused solely on the teen and often begin with the pronoun "you."

DODGE IT!	TRY IT!
Being solution-focused, persuading and saying, *"I understand."*	Showing acceptance. Convey empathy by forming reflections that begin with *"you."*

Chapter Wrap-Up

The purpose of Step 1: Explore (E) is to explore what a teen thinks and feels before you share your own thoughts, feelings, and perspectives. By doing this, you convey acceptance for a teen's point of view and show interest and curiosity for their thoughts, feelings, and experiences. Being successful in this step requires you to be prepared and READY for a conversation with a teen when the time comes. It is extremely important in this step to wear your "listening hat" and listen actively with the intent to understand the teen. Active listening includes asking questions (i.e., open-ended, multiple-choice, and hypothetical questions), showing appreciation for and *seeing* the teen (i.e., saying thanks), affirming their positive aspects (i.e., VASE statements), forming reflections to convey empathy and understanding, and summarizing a teen's story.

Chapter 9

STEP 2: OFFER (O)

*T*he purpose of this step is to convey your message in an effective and respectful way. This step involves packaging or presenting your message in a way that increases a teen's openness, receptivity, desire, and motivation to hear what you have to say. It is about conveying your message in such a way that a teen understands it, and where you are coming from.

Among other things, your message could be about the following.

- Your (or others) perspectives or views.
- Sharing information of knowledge.
- Any concerns.
- Setting limits or boundaries.
- Tips and advice.
- Suggestions and solutions.

As a logical adult with your fully developed pre-frontal cortex, you are responsible for offering information in a way that a teen can understand (See Chapter 2). How you package and deliver your message affects how much the teen hears what you say, listens to you, and takes your information into account. It can be extremely difficult to reach a teen at any point in time if:

- The teen is uninterested or unwilling to listen.
- Focusing or concentrating on other things.
- Feeling tired or sick.
- Under the influence of alcohol or drugs.
- Experiencing strong emotions (i.e., love, anger, sadness, joy).

The goal of the second step is to encourage a teen to take in AND understand your message and hopefully sow the seeds of change (on the teen's part) if necessary.

Packaging your Message

Our openness or motivation to take in information is largely affected by how important the information is to us, as well as our ability and readiness to take it in (Rollnick & Miller, 2013). Our willingness, readiness, and ability to take in information is positively affected when opportunities are created for good conversations. In other words, a positive relationship based on good communication enhances a teen's willingness, readiness, and ability to take in and absorb what an adult has to say to them. This tells us how essential it is to think about how you package and deliver your message so that a teen is open to listening, understanding, and absorbing what you have to say.

WHEN does the teen in your circle open up?

1. **Choose an appropriate time to deliver your message**

It may be worth thinking about the time of day that a teen might be in the best mood to communicate with an adult. For example, talking to a teen when they are in the middle of a video game or in the morning when they are still half asleep, will be ultimately less effective.

Take some time to reflect on what times of the day the teen in your circle functions best and aim as often as possible to choose that time for important conversations. When I want to discuss something with my daughter or see how things are, I often try to do it just before lights out because that is when she opens up the most.

2. Choose an appropriate place to deliver your message

Where a conversation takes place also affects a teen's motivation to take in, listen to, and understand your message. Conversations with teens do not *have* to take place "face to face" at a table. Teens can sometimes feel uncomfortable having conversations in environments which they perceive as stiff, inflexible, or serious. It may be necessary to capture a moment that has spontaneously

arisen. The implication being that adults need to be prepared and READY for whenever the teen opens up. (See Chapter 8). However, despite our best efforts to always be present, our "righting-reflex" takes over too quickly and sometimes we offer solutions where they are not needed nor wanted. If you can relate to this, you are not alone. The key is that you are trying and hopefully can recognize your "oopsie" sooner rather than later. So, I would like to share my latest "oopsie" with you, which happened just this morning with my daughter when her aunt asked her if she wanted to go to the horse stables that afternoon. Here was our short conversation.

Daughter: *Mom, Auntie asked if I wanted to go to the stables.*

Me: *Oh, that's nice. Are you going to go?*

Daughter: *I don't know. I'm worried about what you will do at home alone. I don't want to leave you all by yourself.*

Me: *Oh, don't worry about me. I will be fine. Probably working with Grampa on the book anyway. You go.*

Daughter: *OK*

It wasn't until I was working on this material, later in the afternoon (when my daughter was at the stables with her aunt), that I realized my "oopsie" and was reminded of how easy it can be to put on your "expert hat" and fall into a "problem-solving trap." What I should've done was put on my "listening hat" and explored what my daughter was thinking. Maybe next time ☺! Upon reflection, here is what I would have liked to have said.

Daughter: *Mom, Auntie asked if I wanted to go to the stables.*

Me: *Oh, that's nice. Are you going to go?* (closed question)

Daughter: *I don't know. I'm worried about what you will do home alone. I don't want to leave you at home all by yourself.*

Me: *Oh, how thoughtful of you to think of me. You are such a caring girl. What do you want to do?* (affirm, open question to see what she wants to do)

The above dialogue proves that it is easy for all of us to throw our "listening hats" up into the air like high-school graduates!

 Consider creating opportunities for good conversations when doing other things together (i.e., during a car ride, on a bike ride, on a walk with the dog, when you cook or bake together). Think about which situations the teen in your circle starts opening up and talking the most and try to choose that place/activity as often as possible.

3. Be mindful of your body language

Communication consists of both verbal and non-verbal signals. Most communication is non-verbal, thereby you reveal more about your feelings, thoughts, and attitudes from your body language. What signals you send out during your communication, and how they are perceived by the teen can be crucial to the conversation, and for your relationship (Alberti & Emmons, 2017; Miller & Rollnick, 2013; Gordon, 2019). It may be important to consider the following:

- **Eye contact** - use "warm eyes", a relaxed and steady gaze to show your interest in the teen during your conversation.
- **Posture** - maintain an "open" body position when communicating with a teen. Be aware of any differences in height between you and a teen.
- **Facial expressions** – make sure your face conveys the same message as your words.
- **Tone of voice** - use a tone of voice that matches your words.

4. Put on your "listening hat"

Consider this statement when communicating with a teen, **"Behind every complaint, there is a desire."** What do you think the teen wants or needs?

Try to capture what the teen wants or needs using reflections. Listen to, and mirror back to, the teen what you hear them say. For example, you could say: *"So, what you really want/need is…."* Feel free to read more about listening skills and using a "listening hat" in Chapter 4.

5. Be mindful of the number of words you use

Another tip for increasing the openness of a teen is to reduce the number of words that are used and present your message in smaller doses. Prior to a conversation with a teen, it may be helpful to narrow down and decide on the most important things you want to convey to the teen and how you can best get their attention. Even if you package and present your message in small doses, it may also be helpful to allow the teen some time to digest and reflect on what you have said.

6. Relate your language to the teen's level

Language used in conversations with teens plays an important role with respect to their openness and motivation to absorb your message, as well as the strength of autonomy they may feel. It may be helpful to consider the following:

○ Use the teen's terminology and language

Consider this example. A school counsellor talks to a 15-year-old about his situation at home and what could be improved in that environment.

> School Counsellor: *What do you think needs to change at home?*
>
> Teen: *Ummmm.... .I don't know ... well, I actually need a better network.*
>
> School Counsellor: *Ahhh ... OK ... you would like a better network. Who are you thinking of... a grandma, grandpa or someone else...maybe..?*
>
> Teen: *Nooooo.... .I mean, we have internet at home but the connection is so slow.*

Even though the school counsellor and the teen were communicating, they still were not speaking the same language. Sound familiar?

Thomas Gordon (2019) describes three common errors that often occur in communication between people. They are:

- The teen does not say what they mean.
- The adult does not *hear* the teen's words correctly.
- The adult misinterprets the teen's words or gives them a different meaning than what was intended.

Using the teen's own terminology and language as much as possible is a good way to avoid these three common communication mistakes and to ensure that the words used mean the same for both you and the teen.

○ **Avoid terminology or words that may negatively affect your "team spirit"**

Put yourself in a teen's position when an adult expresses the following:

"You never help out."

"What have you done?"

"You always get mad when I am only trying to help."

"You should…"

"You really have to start thinking more about…"

"You are with your friends all the time."

"Thanks for the help but next time do it right when you get home."

It is important to avoid phrases or words that generalize, for example **never, always** or **all the time**, as well as words such as **but, must, should**. These words can trigger an argument and put someone on the defensive immediately, as well as negatively affecting your relationship with them. When conversing with teens, saying these words may lead to them feeling bad or inadequate.

Instead, using "tentative (or cautious) language" can be helpful to soften your communication and allowing the teen to absorb your message more easily (LaRock, 2019). The purpose of tentative or cautious language is to convey to the teen that your message (i.e., idea or opinion) is not necessarily the "be-all, end-all" and that there may be other aspects you have not yet considered (i.e., a teen's idea, perspective, or opinion). Tentative language helps you avoid generalizations and assumptions about the teen, keeping your "expert hat" on the hat rack. Using this language with a teen tones down any frustration or resistance in the conversation and conveys that you are trying to listen carefully to the teen's perspective allowing space for change to occur. Proofreading Academy (2020) provides the following examples of tentative language.

Appear to be	Eventually	Possibly/probably
Can/could	Often	Seems
Generally	Some	Perhaps
May/might		

Other helpful words and phrases that can create "team spirit," convey compassion, demonstrate a positive focus, and show acceptance are:

> *"You are unsure about…"*
>
> *"For the most part…"*
>
> *"Sometimes…"*
>
> *"…a little…"*
>
> *"It's not really what you expected…"*
>
> *"It seems like…"*
>
> *"It can be…"*
>
> *"And at the same time…"*
>
> *"Right now…"*

In conclusion, it can be important to think about the language you use in conversations with a teen because the language used can encourage a teen's willingness to listen to, absorb, and understand your message.

Packaging your Message Wrap-up

There are several things that you can consider when communicating with a teen and delivering your intended message. These tips intend to create a good conversational environment and increase the teen's receptivity to hear, listen to, and absorb what you have to say.

Delivering your Message

Consider this situation. You arrive home to find a jacket lying on the floor in the hallway. It's been a long day; you are feeling tired and frustrated. With irritation in your voice, you inadvertently catch the teen's attention by asking a little too loudly, *"Do you always have to throw your jacket on the floor? How hard can it be to just hang it up when you get home?"*

Feel free to reflect on this situation using the questions below.

- What do you think the teen hears you say?
- How do you think this makes the teen feel?
- How receptive, or motivated, do you think the teen will be to hanging up their jacket the next time?

Would it have made a difference if instead you had said, *"I would appreciate it if you could hang your jacket in the closet right away when you get home, instead of leaving it on the floor"?*

I-messages

One way to express yourself is to use I-messages. An I-message involves using the pronoun "I" when you express yourself, for example, *"I would appreciate…"* or *"I'm worried about…"*

An I-message makes it clear to the other person that you are conveying **your** subjective experiences, perceptions, thoughts, feelings, wishes, and desires in a situation. Expressing yourself using I-messages means that you take responsibility for these subjective reactions instead of passing them on to the other person (Miller (2018), Gordon (1970), Alberti, R & Emmons, M. (2017)). The opposite of I-messages are "you–messages" which shift the focus from you to the person you are talking to, for example *"you are always late," "you don't listen"* or *"you drive me crazy."* See the illustration of I-messages below.

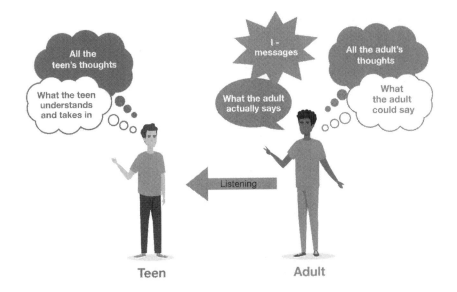

Let's take a moment and clarify when you can use the word "you" in your communications with a teen. In MI, we use the pronoun "you" to respectfully convey to another person that they are the complete focus of the conversation. This is done when we, among other things, want to show appreciation for a person (i.e., *"Thank you for helping me"*), affirm someone (i.e., *"You are a brave girl"*), or convey empathy by forming reflections (i.e., *"It is important for you to be understood"*). Reflections are discussed in detail in Chapter 8.

When the purpose of the conversation is to deliver a message from your own perspective, it is much more respectful to focus on your own experience by using I-messages, instead of using the word "you." For example, *"you spend all your money on energy drinks."*

There are several benefits to using I-messages in conversations with teens. I-messages can:

- Make it easier for a teen to listen to and absorb your message.
- Minimize the risk that a teen feels accused of something, criticized, or blamed.

- Minimize the risk that a teen will become defensive and prepare for a verbal counterattack.

- Encourage teens to be ready, willing, and able to act differently in the future.

- Pave the way for open and effective communication with a teen.

- Convey respect for the teen and show that you care about the teen's feelings.

- Help you be a role model to the teen by showing that you are actively thinking about how you package and present your message.

Now that you are familiar with some of the benefits of using I-messages, let's take a closer look at recognizing the differences between you-messages and I-messages.

You-messages	I-messages
"You are not listening to me."	*"I would like to be listened to."*
"You are driving me crazy."	*"I feel frustrated."*
"You are so annoying!"	*"I feel irritated and do not know what to do about it."*

It is important to realize that not every message beginning with the pronoun "I" is an I-message. Unfortunately, some I-messages can include a cleverly disguised you-message causing the message to sound accusatory without meaning or intending to. An example of this is when a message includes the word "that". When the word "that" is used, it becomes easier for the pronoun "you" to sneak in too (i.e., *"I really feel that **you** are getting angry over nothing"* or *"I think that **you** need to take some responsibility for your school work"*). See how in these examples, the focus is deflected from your **subjective** experience and opinion of the situation onto the other person. Using an I-message would sound more like, *"I would like to understand your perspective and discuss this calmly"* or *"I would like to help share the responsibility of your school work"*. Think back to the description of Thomas Gordon's (1970) listening process presented earlier (See Chapter 8).

HELPFUL TIPS   Trust in the spirit of MI by establishing a relationship based on "team spirit," a positive teen focus, acceptance whilst supporting the teen's autonomy (See Chapter 6).

Exercise: I-messages

Objective: To practice forming I-messages and to become familiar with the different ways I-messages can be expressed in a situation.

Instructions: Read the examples below and form I-messages that could be used to convey your message to a teen in a conversation. After you have written your own suggestions, reflect on some other suggestions.

Example 1: "You must understand that when there are people about who offer drugs to teens, you should not hang out in the schoolyard where they are."

I-message

Suggestion:

"Given that there are people selling drugs to teens in the schoolyard, I'm worried about you."

Example 2: "You always get so angry when I'm just trying to help you."

I-message

_____

_____

_____

Suggestion:

"I feel sad when I cannot help you."

Example 3: "Thanks for the help. But next time, do it right away when you get home."

I-message

_____

_____

_____

Suggestion:

"Thanks for the help. I would appreciate if it was done right away next time."

Your example:

_____

_____

_____

I-message

_____

_____

_____

Your example:

_____

_____

_____

I-message

_____

_____

_____

Self-reflection

- What did the exercise encourage you to think about?
- How can you incorporate this in your everyday interactions with the teen?

When using I-messages, it is essential to keep track of your non-verbal signals and body language. These can be but aren't limited to your facial expressions, posture, and tone of voice. By being aware of these, you are more likely to avoid a disguised, and unintentional, accusation in your message.

Exercise: I-messages

Objective: To practice using I-messages in a conversation with a teen.

Instructions – Part 1: Choose a positive (or neutral) behaviour or situation that you would like to discuss with a teen in your circle using I-messages. If you feel comfortable doing so, think about and prepare what you would like to say in advance. When you are ready, engage the teen in the conversation.

Self-reflection

- How do you feel the conversation went?
- What new things did you learn about the teen?
- What important things did you hear the teen say?
- How can you incorporate this in your everyday interactions with the teen?

Instructions – Part 2: Choose a more challenging behaviour or situation that you would like to discuss with a teen using I-messages. If you feel comfortable doing so, think about and prepare what you would like to say in advance. When you are ready, engage the teen in the conversation.

Self-reflection

- How do you feel the conversation went?
- What new things did you learn about the teen?
- What important things did you hear the teen say?
- How can you incorporate this in your everyday interactions with the teen?

Three-part Communication Model

Good communication is necessary to collaborate with a teen to allow you to dance together instead of wrestle. For some people, learning a dance routine is easier if the steps are structured or choreographed and they can follow a lead. Structure and I-messages can help ensure that the teen understands your intended message. It may be useful when it is necessary to express both your needs and desires in an effective and assertive way, while at the same time respecting the teen's needs and desires.

The following *Three-part Communication Model* (choreography) was inspired by literature, articles, and books pertaining to I-messages, assertive communication, social skills training, active listening, Motivational Interviewing (MI) and Cognitive Behavioural Therapy (CBT)[4]. Here are the three parts:

1. **Describe the other person's behaviour or the situation as objectively as possible.**

   "When _____ happens ..."

   "When I see..."

---

[4] Miller (2018); Miller & Rollnick (2013); Alberti & Emmons (2017); Gordon, T. (2019), Homeland Office England, Steps for Health, Goldstein, A., Glick, B. & Gibbs, J. (1998); Glick, B. & Gibbs, J (2011).

When describing a situation, it can sometimes be difficult to express yourself objectively and keep your emotions in check. Consider the following example.

You have agreed on a curfew with a teen in your circle, but the teen comes home late. When the teen finally comes through the door, you say impatiently, "*I am really disappointed that you are late. We agreed on a time for you to be home!*"

Depending on how strong your relationship ("team spirit") is with the teen, this I-message can miss the mark. A teen may interpret this as an accusation and feel blamed. After all, if the teen had come home on time, you would not have any reason to feel disappointed?

What difference would it make if the message had been expressed like this: "*We agreed on a time for you to be here and that agreement was broken.*"

It feels different, right? When possible, try to formulate your I-messages without using the pronoun "you" at all. This way, the focus is completely on your subjective opinion being expressed in an objective manner, while avoiding any unintentional blame or accidental guilt trips.

It can be difficult to formulate I-messages, especially when talking with a teen. Strong emotions can overwhelm you and make it harder to be objective. It can also be difficult to know exactly what to say or spontaneously come up with the right words. This is normal, very common, and completely OK! Take a moment to calm down and allow yourself time to work out the best non-emotional response. If you feel comfortable, try jotting down your thoughts and feelings or practice formulating your response objectively with the help of someone you trust.

2. Describe how the other person's behaviour or the situation affects you and makes you feel.

Continuing with an objective description, it may be useful to think about and formulate how the other person's behaviour or situation has affected you, without jumping directly into describing your feelings. Describing your feelings will be covered a little bit later within this book. For example, you may have difficulty concentrating or being confident when experiencing the other person's behaviour or the situation.

"This affects me because I…"

"I am negatively affected by…"

"_____ happens to me."

"I get tongue-tied and cannot find words to explain what I mean."

"I get confused."

"I lose my self-confidence."

After you have reflected over and formulated how the other person's behaviour or the situation has affected you, you can now turn your attention to your feelings. How does the other person's behaviour or the situation make you feel? When describing your feelings, it can be helpful to remember the basic human emotions: anger, fear, disgust, sadness, and happiness (Ekman, 1992).

"I feel sad / angry / scared / happy…"

"I'm worried that something is going to happen to you."

3. Provide an alternative suggestion for future situations.

It is much easier for another person to listen to and absorb your message if it comes in the form of a well thought out and respectful suggestion.

"I would like to…"

"It could help me if we…"

"I would appreciate it if…"

"I really need to…"

"It would be helpful for me if…"

Example – Putting it all together

"We agreed on a time that you would be home, and that agreement was broken (1). I feel disappointed about that and I started worrying that something had happened to you (2). I would really appreciate a heads up (like a phone call) in the future if you're going to be late (3)."

In keeping with the spirit of MI, and the importance of your "team spirit", it is necessary to invite feedback about your message from the teen. We will discuss how you can do this in Chapter 10.

Exercise: Three-part Communication Model

Objective: To practice using a communication model, read some suggestions and see and understand the different ways the three-part communication model can be expressed in a situation.

Instructions: Write down suggestions of how you could convey your message to the teen in the examples below using the communication model. Then read some suggestions.

Example 1: Ebba is 14 years old and does not do her chores at a time that you would like her to. You often come home after a long tiring day at work to find the kitchen in disarray and that Ebba has not emptied the dishwasher.

Use the model:

_____

_____

_____

_____

Suggestion:

"When I come home tired after work and the dishwasher is not emptied (1), I feel annoyed (2). So, I would appreciate it if the dishwasher were unloaded before I get home (3)."

Example 2: Anna is a 17-year-old girl who places very high demands on herself. She feels that she needs to be good at most things, and has a hard time dealing with things when they do not match her expectations. Right now, she feels bad about not knowing what to do after finishing high school and on top of that, she is stressed about her school grades.

Use the model:

....

....

....

....

Suggestion:

"It seems that you place very high demands on yourself when it comes to school. I see a girl who wants to be good at lots of things (1) and I get worried about how that makes you feel (2). I would like us to talk about it and how I could help you (3)."

Example 3: You are the mother of 14-year-old Simon who divides his time between living with you and his father. You and Simon's dad have a hard time communicating with each other about summer plans and living arrangements. Simon feels that he often ends up in the middle of these conflicts, and it is noticeable that they have a negative effect on him. He is often sad, tired, and grumpy.

Use the model:

....

....

....

....

Suggestion:

"When your dad and I have a hard time communicating about the summer/ housing/other things, it affects us all (1). I'm sorry that this makes you feel this way (2) and I wish I could influence the situation more than I do (3)."

"I see that you are affected/saddened by the fact that your father and I cannot communicate better (1). I feel both sad and frustrated that this is the case (2). I wish it were different for you (3)."

Example 4: Julia is 16 years old and does not seem to be herself anymore. She is becoming quieter and more withdrawn over time. She does not want to talk to you about what is bothering her and has started cutting her arms. You are concerned and want to talk to her about it while at the same time are aware that she is in a fragile state and you do not want to risk pushing her away.

Use the model:

_____

_____

_____

_____

Suggestion:

"It seems to me that you are not really doing so well (1). I'm worried about you (2). I would like us to talk about it when you feel ready, and I will do my best to give you the right support (3)."

Example 5: David is a 15-year-old who likes to play computer games. He has many friends in the virtual world and is well known for his gaming. In the beginning, David was able to balance his gaming with other activities. However, now playing computer games has started to take over his everyday life and is having a negative effect on him. His schooling is suffering, and he is exercising less. David is often in a bad mood and as he inverts his sleep pattern, he often loses track of time and plays late into the night.

Use the model:

....

....

....

....

Suggestion:

"It appears that you are spending a lot of time in front of the computer and this has started to affect your school work, your health and your mood (1). I feel frustrated and anxious at the same time (2). I would like us to talk about this to help you find some balance again (3)."

Example 6: Elijah is 14 years old and finds it difficult to go back to school after the weekends and when there have been study days. He cannot put into words why he feels this way. You would like to express your concern for him and the potential impact on his schooling.

Use the model:

....

....

....

....

Suggestion:

"I notice that after the weekends, it hard for you to go back to school (1). It's hard for me to see you struggling to get going and I'm worried about you and your future at school (2). I would like us to talk to your mentor about it together and see how we can help you (3)."

Self-reflection

- What did the exercise encourage you to think about?
- How can you incorporate this in your everyday interactions with the teen?

Exercise: Three-part Communication Model

Objective: To practice using the Three-part Communication Model in your everyday interactions with a teen.

Instructions: Choose something that you would like to talk to the teen in your circle about. Think about and prepare what you would like to say in advance. When you are ready, engage the teen in the conversation using the Three-part Communication Model.

Self-reflection

- How do you feel the conversation went?
- What new things did you learn about the teen?
- What important things did you hear the teen say?
- How can you incorporate this in your everyday interactions with the teen?

Delivering your Message Wrap-up

Using *I-messages* and/or the *Three-part Communication Model* are two ways of formulating your message when you would like to talk to a teen about something sensitive or important. Without being critical of the teen in question, you convey your perspective while actively showing respect for how your message could be received by them. You express yourself in a way that allows you to both take responsibility for your own feelings, thoughts, and experiences, as well as inform the teen of your desires and needs. The teen hears and can absorb your message more easily without feeling that they are being accused of something.

DODGE IT!	TRY IT!
You-messages.	Deliver your message with respect.
Language that can give an accusatory impression or guilt-trip.	Use I-messages or the Three-part Communication Model.

Supporting a Teen's Autonomy

Chapter 5 addressed the three basic psychological needs – the need for autonomy, competence, and relatedness. The need for autonomy is a teen's need to feel free to make their own decisions and influence their own lives. Supporting and promoting autonomy involves conveying acceptance of a teen's choices, not necessarily liking those choices. Supporting a teen's autonomy means conveying that you want the teen to feel that they *can* make their own decisions, within defined boundaries. This also means recognizing a teen's *right* to agree or disagree, to like your information/message or not, and to choose for themselves what they want to believe in or how they want to act.

There are some situations in life where it is difficult for anyone to choose with complete freedom. For example, a teen cannot choose whether (or not) to attend school or whether (or not) to take prescribed diabetic medication. However, even in situations where their choices may be limited, a teen can be engaged to influence their choices within those defined boundaries (Naar-King & Suarez, 2011).

An example of supporting autonomy in such a situation might sound like this, *"Attending school is not something you can choose. You can of course be involved in outlining your individual study plan and choosing what you want that plan to look like."* A more general attempt to support and promote a teen's autonomy might sound like this, *"When would it be a good time to talk about _____?"*

Although this book does touch briefly on situations where teens have limited options and how to engage a teen and support their autonomy in those situations, it mainly focuses on situations where teens have genuine and obvious options to choose from.

Use Language that Supports a Teen's Autonomy

Your language can promote or undermine a person's autonomy. Language that supports and promotes autonomy involves identifying and verbalizing a teen's options and choices, sense of control, and personal responsibility (Dixelius & Ljunggren, 2019). Language used to support or promote autonomy often uses the pronoun "you." For example:

> *"This may not feel right to you…"*
>
> *"I'm here to listen and to find out what you make of………"*
>
> *"It really is up to you, which choice you make."*
>
> *"You're at a crossroads. You really are the one who knows what works the best for you."*
>
> *"You made your own decision! You could have smoked like your friends did, but you chose to stick to your guns and say no."*

Emphasize Choice

All people have a basic need to feel free, make their own choices, and influence their own lives. However, this basic need for autonomy does not necessarily mean that people can live their lives however they want, without being affected by the consequences of those choices. We all live within a context (society or environment) with cultural and social frameworks that we need to take into consideration when we make decisions. Within that framework, there are often options one can choose from and decide. The options may not be obvious, such as an easy choice between "great option A" and "bad option B." Some situations, present choices between "bad option B" and an "even worse option C." By identifying and exploring all options available to a teen (with curiosity and neutrality), you emphasize choice by discussing the options within the teen's context and framework. For example, language that supports autonomy in these situations might sound something like, *"You may choose between "X" and "Y". What do you think is best for you?"*

Let's return to the example of increasing my son's motivation to attend the extra English classes. Below, is an example of how our interaction sounded when I attempted to support his autonomy by emphasizing choices.

Son: *Mom, do I have to go to English today. It's sooooo boring!*

Me: *Yes, of course, you have to. You know that. Do we have to have this same conversation every week?* (set boundaries, closed question)

Son: *But Moooom……why? Nobody thinks it's fun!*

Me: *Ian…can I ask you something?* (ask permission = support autonomy)

Son: "nods"

Me: *… when you realize that tomorrow is Monday and that you have English, what thoughts pop into your head?* (open-ended question)

Son: *Like … 'I want to die', 'it's super boring', 'I don't want to go'… how many more do you want?*

Me: *Hmmm … you have some really negative thoughts when you think about English. Can I ask you something?* (affirm, ask permission = support autonomy)

Son: *Yes …*

Me: *With those thoughts floating around in your head, how much "fun" do you think it will be to go to English?* (open-ended question)

Son: *Exactly! I don't want to go to English. Do I have to?*

Me: *Yes, English is important. In what ways do you think it is important for you to go to English?* (set boundaries, open-ended question)

Son: *Moooooom ………(sigh) …… so I can get better at speaking English.*

Me: *That's right ... speaking better English is important to you. How come you want to get better at English?* (reflection, open-ended question)

Son: *So, I can talk to Grammy and Grampy and all those people in Canada. So, I can study there and get my driver's license when I'm 16. So...ummm...I can get a job there and make money.*

Me: *Wow! You have lots of reasons to improve your English. Can I ask you something else?* (affirm, reflection, ask for permission = support autonomy)

Son: *Fine....*

Me: *How could reminding yourself of those reasons help you when you realize that you have to go to your extra English class?* (open-ended question)

Son: *Uhhhh ... huh!?*

Me: *I mean...could you maybe stop and think..."hmmm.... English can help me when I go to school and get my driver's license in Canada" instead of "English is boring?"* (closed question seeking a direct answer)

Son: *Maybe....*

Me: *Because we have talked about that fact...(pause)...that quitting the extra English classes is not an option. But you can definitely choose what thoughts you pay attention to when you think about going there...I mean, if you think positively or negatively about it.... (pause)...What do you think about that...(pause)...that you can choose your mindset before the lesson?* (set boundaries, emphasize choice = support autonomy, open-ended question)

Son: *Yeah, I knnoooooowwwww. But it's still boring.*

Me: *Maybe it is, and will continue to be boring if you choose to continue thinking of English class as the worst thing in the world.... (pause)....What do you make of all this?* (affirm, open-ended question)

Son: *I'll try...*

What do you think? Did the conversation above feel more like a wrestling match or a dance where we moved together, back and forth, towards a common solution?

Encourage and Emphasize Personal Responsibility

There are situations where you may want to both emphasize a teen's choices, as well as actively collaborate with a teen throughout the decision-making process. By doing this, you assist a teen in making well-informed decisions, as well as decisions that they will hopefully be ready, willing, and able to take responsibility for. By having these types of discussions with a teen, you help them think critically and creatively about their choices, which in turn encourages them to be responsible and independent individuals (Williams, 2002; Naar-King & Suarez, 2011). Conversations of this sort can include discussing and considering alternatives and consequences and examining choices in relation to a teen's values.

Alternatives and Consequences

One way to encourage a teen to take personal responsibility is to help the teen verbalize from their own perspective the alternatives they see and the consequences that exist for each alternative. Here are some tips.

- What are the advantages and disadvantages or each alternative?
- What are the short- and long-term consequences of each alternative?
- What choices do you have?

After you have considered all alternatives and their consequences together with the teen, it may be helpful to summarize the important gold nuggets from the discussion. Encourage the teen to decide what is best for them, while at the same time taking responsibility for any consequences arising from that decision.

Exercise: Talking about Consequences

Objective: To practice discussing alternatives and consequences with a teen.

Instructions: Choose an example or theme from your daily interactions with a teen in your circle that you would like to talk to them about. Using a pen and paper, feel free to use the table provided to discuss the positive consequences and the less positive consequences, consider them both in the short and long term. Examples of everyday themes to discuss are quitting sports, smoking cigarettes, coming home on time or getting up in time for school.

Helpful tool: Table of Alternatives and Consequences

Alternative	In the Near Future	In the Long Run
Positive		
Less Positive		

Self-reflection

- How do you feel the conversation went?
- What new things did you learn about the teen?
- What important things did you hear the teen say?
- How can you incorporate this in your everyday interactions with the teen?

Teen choices in relation to their values

Another way to encourage a teen to take responsibility for their situation, life or behaviour is to discuss them in relation to that individual teen's values (Naar-King & Suarez, 2011). Together with the teen, identify and explore what they consider personally important and how those values are affected by their current behaviour or situation. Feel free to return to Chapter 3 for a detailed description of how to explore a teen's values.

○ **Acknowledge and affirm what is important to the teen**

   "You want to live a long life."

   "You would like to do this for your own sake and not someone else's."

   "It is important to you to…"

○ **Ask open-ended questions, in a non-judgmental and respectful manner**

   "What is most important to you right now?"

   "What does …(value)…mean to you?"

   "How does your smoking fit together with you wanting to live a long and healthy life?"

   "How does your difficulty getting up in the morning fit together with you wanting to attend a high school with a hockey program?"

Chapter Wrap-Up

Step 2: Offer (O) aims to deliver your message and to present that message in a way that increases a teen's openness to listening and taking in what you have to say within a conversation. This step considers when, where, and how your message would be best conveyed. When delivering your message, your body language and choice of words are crucial. Helpful tips for success are to wear your "listening hat" and convey the spirit of MI ("team-spirit," compassion, acceptance, positive focus), even though in this step, you are the one expressing yourself and delivering a message.

This step includes two ways in which to express yourself. The first way is using I-messages to deliver your information while taking personal responsibility for your own subjective experiences, thoughts, and feelings. The second way includes using a more structured model, the Three-part Communication Model, to ensure that your message is as objective as possible, thereby promoting the receptivity of the teen. In this step, using a language that supports and promotes autonomy, identifies, and emphasizes the choices available, and encourages the teen to take personal responsibility, all contribute to a teen's willingness, ability, and readiness to take in what you have to say.

Chapter 10

STEP 3: EXPLORE (E)

*S*ydney J. Harris, an American author and journalist, compared the terms *information* and *communication*. He wrote that these two words are often used interchangeably but that they in fact have very different meanings. More specifically, Harris said that *"information is giving out, communication is getting through"*
(Rollnick, S., Kaplan, S. & Rutschman, R., 2016, pg.63). The latter is what the conversational tool Explore-Offer-Explore (EOE) is designed to help with improving your communication with a teen and "getting through" directly to them.

By using EOE to communicate with a teen, you have explored their perspective and actively listened using the conversational tools presented (Step 1: Explore (E)). You have packaged, presented, and delivered your message with kindness, compassion, and respect using *I-messages* and/or the *Three-part Communication Model*. You have even consciously packaged and presented your message to support and promote the teen's autonomy (Step 2: Offer (O)). Now the questions you need to consider are:

- How do you know that the teen has heard you?
- How do you know that you and the teen have understood each other?

- How can you be sure that your message has actually "gotten through" to the teen?

In the last step of EOE (Step 3: Explore (E)), it is important to check in with the teen and get answers to the questions above. Again, it can also be very helpful in this step to put on your "listening hat" and remind yourself of Thomas Gordon's listening process and the importance of closing the circle of communication to make sure that you understand each other (See Chapter 8).

Step 3: Explore (E) has two aims. The first aim involves seeing what the teen has heard you say and checking the teen's cognitive understanding of your message. In other words, Step 3: Explore (E) sees what sense the teen makes of your message. It gives you and the teen the chance to reflect on your message together, ask further questions of each other, understand the teen's reactions to your message, and, if necessary, correct any misunderstandings. The second aim of this step is to further explore the teen's perspective regarding your message and determine possible steps towards change together.

It is just as important in this last step to be READY to communicate with the teen, actively listen, and demonstrate the spirit of MI. A strong "team spirit" is needed in this step, as well as acceptance of the teen's perspective, compassion and understanding of the teen's needs, and seeing the teen as a distinct individual with their own internal strengths and resources.

Aim #1: Check the Teen's Understanding and Get Feedback

To explore what the teen has heard you say, as well as the teen's cognitive understanding of your message, it can be helpful to engage in the following.

- Wear your "listening hat" and use the **helpful steps to enhance your listening skills.**

- Ask the teen to summarize in their own words what they have heard and understood.

  "Could you please summarize what you heard me say?"

  "Please, tell me what the point of my information was."

- Show interest and accept the teen's point of view.

- Support and promote the teen's autonomy both verbally and non-verbally.

- Have a positive focus.

- Be affirming and use VASE to form affirmations.

- Ask questions to understand the teen's perspective.

  "What do you think about...?"

  "How does that sound to you?"

  "What do you make of all this?"

- Summarize the conversation.

Aim #2: Explore the Teen's Perspective

In addition to determining the teen's cognitive understanding of your message, it is also important to explore their thoughts on a more emotional level. In this way, you get a greater insight into what the teen thinks and feels about what you have said, how your message has affected them, and what the teen is going to do with the knowledge gained from your message. In other words, the focus here is to see how the teen will "integrate" your message into their own thoughts and behaviour, as well as to see how they intend to incorporate this information in the future. It can therefore be helpful to engage in the following.

- Wear your "listening hat" and use the **helpful steps to enhance your listening skills.**

- Show interest and accept the teen's point of view.
- Support and promote the teen's autonomy both verbally and non-verbally.
- Have a positive focus.
- Be affirming and use VASE to form affirmations.
- Ask questions to understand the teen's perspective.

  "How does this information affect you?"

  "What feelings arise when you hear this information?"

  "What does hearing what I said mean to you?"

  "How does hearing what I said fit into your life?"

  "What does all this mean to you?"

  "What do you make of the information/what I have told you?"

  "How do you see this?"

  "What do you feel knowing this information?"

- Summarize the conversation.

There are many questions that can be used to explore a teen's thoughts and feelings about your message. Choose the question or questions that suit you and the teen in your circle best or brainstorm your own questions which may be better suited to your daily interactions with the teen.

The Road Ahead

In some situations, or conversations, it may be enough for you and the teen to have reached a common understanding of each other's perspectives. You have actively listened, explored the teen's point of view, and received feedback (this step's first aim). Next, you explored what the teen made of your message and discussed possible steps the teen will consider towards change (this step's second aim). As a result, you are both satisfied with the outcome of the conversation. Always make a conscious effort to remember to thank the teen for their time and for sharing their point of view.

However, in other situations or conversations, it may be that your message contained a more definite suggestion or request for change, for example you would like the teen to act differently in the future. It can then be important to collaborate with the teen to find a shared way forward and act as a guide while the teen verbalizes their next step. Examples of such goals or changes might be:

- Meeting curfew.
- Doing homework without complaining.
- Applying coping strategies to handle anxiety.
- Doing homework every day.
- Continuing with a sport or leisure activity.
- Being kinder to siblings.
- Consuming fewer energy drinks.

Exercise: Towards Change

Objective: To practice using open-ended questions to increase a teen's motivation for change.

Instructions: Engage a teen in a conversation about their goals and the way forward to reach those goals. Feel free to use the "Towards Change Cheat Sheet" found at https://en.novovia.se/bookresources. Listen actively to what the teen has to say. Wear your "listening hat" and use the **helpful steps to enhance your listening skills.**

1. **Explore** using open-ended questions
   - Based on what you are thinking now, what changes are you considering making?
   - How important do you think it is for you to make a change?

- What do you hope to gain by making a change?
- What are your three most important reasons for making a change?
- What difference are you hoping this change will lead to?
- Which of your positive qualities do you plan to use to be successful in this change?
- Based on what we have talked about, what do you think your next step will be?

2. **Summarize**: Form a very short summary (approx. 20 sec) to capture the teen's *main reasons* for making this change.

3. **Ask:** What do you think you will do now?

Self-reflection

- How do you feel the conversation went?
- What new things did you learn about the teen?
- What important things did you hear the teen say?
- How can you incorporate this in your everyday interactions with the teen?

Planning help - BAP

A "Brief Action Plan", or BAP[5], is a practical tool to help a teen set both bigger and smaller goals. BAP is a quick and easy plan in four steps.

Step 1: What do you want? What is your goal?

What would you like to change within the next few weeks?

 Make sure that your goal is specific, realistic, achievable, and important to the teen.

---

[5] Developed by Steven Cole, Damara Gutnick, Connie Davis, and Kathy Reims, www.centreCMI.ca. Modified by Jennifer Ollis Blomqvist for the purposes of this book.

Step 2: Make a plan

How? Where? When?

Step 3: Implement your plan

How confident do you feel about carrying out your plan?

What is needed for you to feel even more confident?

Step 4: Follow up your plan

When would you like to review how things are going with your plan?

How did it go with the plan?

Handling a Teen's Feedback

If you are not used to getting feedback from a teen, it can feel unusual, or even a bit awkward. Although you can present your message in the best way you know how to, you cannot be completely sure how your message is going to be received. Even if you have made the effort to plan and deliver your message respectfully, it does not automatically mean that the teen will thank you for it, like it, accept or believe it. Don't forget that you always have your "listening hat" to wear and MI's spirit and conversational style to lean on.

We will now turn to handling feedback from a teen, from both sides, depending on whether the teen's reaction/response is what you expected or not.

An Expected Reaction

If the teen's response to your message is what you expected, and without emotional storms or conflict, it may be worthwhile to take a few minutes and reflect on that. Ask yourself the following questions to help reflect on the teen's feedback.

- How does it feel to get the expected result?
- What did you do to make the conversation successful?

- In your communications with the teen, what was useful to achieve this result?

An Unexpected Reaction

Communication can be difficult and unexpected or unwanted outcomes may occur, for example conflicts, expression of strong feelings, misunderstandings, or misconceptions. If these reactions happen, it is important to go easy on yourself. Show yourself kindness and understanding and remain focused on your efforts to get through to a teen you care about. It can be necessary, and extremely helpful, to build up your strength and positive energy when you try again (See Part Three).

 If you have tried and received an unexpected reaction, then you may feel disappointed and frustrated. I can share a tip that has been useful for me when my conversations did not go as I had hoped or expected. My tip is to use the social skill steps for "Responding to Failure" developed by Goldstein, Glick & Gibbs (1998).

1. Decide if you have failed at something.
2. Think about why you failed.
3. Think about what you could do to keep from failing another time.
4. Decide if you want to try again.
5. Try again using your new idea.

Chapter Wrap-Up

Step 3: Explore (E) is the final step in the EOE tool and is crucial for further communication with a teen. This step includes following up by checking the teen's understanding of your message, as well as getting feedback regarding the teen's thoughts and feelings about the message you presented in Step 2: Offer (O). In this step, handling the feedback that you receive from the teen is very important. This step also allows for further guidance of a teen towards change if the teen shows signs of readiness. A Brief Action Plan (BAP) can be used to discuss and set goals together with the teen to help them move forward.

DODGE IT!	TRY IT!
Getting caught up in an emotional storm.	Check understanding, get feedback and explore the teen's perspective.
	Set goals using a Brief Action Plan (BAP).

Part Three

Self-Care

Chapter 11

IMPORTANCE OF SELF-CARE

*W*hen discussing self-care, I think about the safety instructions provided before a plane takes off. Anyone who has flown *and* listened to the safety instructions knows that in the event of a change in cabin pressure (perhaps due to turbulence), you are supposed to put on your own oxygen mask first BEFORE helping another person put on their mask. I mean, what good would it do if you passed out trying to help someone else get their mask on? Now the other person is in a tough situation and most likely will pass out too. It really does make sense. Take good care of yourself first before trying to help someone else.

Interactions and conversations with teens can be everything from wonderful, inspiring, and fun, to challenging, frightening, and sometimes worrisome. Life with teens, with all its' ups and downs, can be thought of as riding an emotional rollercoaster or experiencing turbulence during a plane ride. Therefore, it is important to take care of yourself first so you can be at your best when you are communicating with a teen.

So here is an important question for you: What does "self-care" mean to you?

Self-care includes, but is not limited to, taking care of yourself physically, emotionally, and psychologically. There are many things you can do to take care of yourself and you probably already have a few ideas that work for you. Part three contains tips for behavioural strategies, exercises, and techniques that can recharge your batteries.

- Increasing positivity in your life.
- Developing proper breathing and relaxation techniques to reduce the effects of stress on your mind and body.
- Coping effectively with feelings and emotions.
- Showing yourself kindness.
- Engaging in relaxing and energizing leisure time.
- Obtaining social and emotional support from others.
- Reducing unhelpful thinking patterns and developing more helpful thinking patterns.

Exercise: Recharging Your Batteries

Objective: To reflect on how you take care of yourself and on the different ways in which you recharge your batteries.

Instructions: Take some time to reflect on the meaning of "self-care" and "recharging your batteries" and on the different ways you have previously used to recharge. Feel free to use the following questions to guide your reflection.

- What does it mean to you to "recharge your batteries"?
- When you are "recharged" how do you feel? Do you feel calm and relaxed or energized and alive?
- What activities have you previously participated in to help recharge your batteries?

Self-reflection

- How did the exercise go?
- In what way is recharging your batteries important to you?

- What would you like to continue doing more of?

Strategies for self-care and for recharging your batteries are individual and work differently for different people. Therefore, it is important for you to discover and use the strategies that work best for your personality and needs. Some examples where you can recharge your batteries include the following.

- Physical exercise.
- Eating and sleeping properly.
- Expressing creativity.
- Playing musical instruments.
- Spending time with family and friends.
- Reading or listening to books, music, or podcasts.
- Practicing yoga.
- Spending time in nature.
- Meditating.
- Practicing breathing and relaxation techniques.

Chapter Wrap-Up

Are you ready to recharge your batteries? This chapter covered:

- An introduction to the idea of self-care.
- The importance of taking care of yourself physically, emotionally, and psychologically.
- Many different strategies for self-care that could work for you.

Chapter 12

INCREASE POSITIVITY IN YOUR LIFE

*I*ncreasing positivity is about much more than just trying to be *positive*. Barbara Fredrickson's (2011) Broaden and Build Theory of Positive Emotions is about the science of positive emotions and is based on two core truths: (1) positive emotions "open our hearts and our minds, making us more receptive and creative" (Fredrickson, 2011, pg. 21) and (2) encourage us to "discover and build new skills, new ties, new knowledge, and new ways of being" (Fredrickson, 2011, pg. 24). This enables us to see new possibilities and bounce back faster from hardships and perceived defeat. Fredrickson's research focuses on genuinely and sincerely experiencing the ten specific forms of positive emotions: joy, gratitude, serenity, interest, hope, pride, amusement, inspiration, awe, and love (Fredrickson, 2011). Fredrickson's research indicates that experiencing these positive emotions versus negative emotions at a 3-to-1 ratio leads people to achieve their goals, improve their performance, and increase their well-being.

Positivity, according to Fredrickson (2011), optimizes how our minds and body's function and is the doorway for greater health, better relationships, improved resiliency, and overall success in life. This chapter focuses on self-care and being "the best" you can be for a teen in your circle. Therefore, increasing positivity in *your* life can be a good way for you to put on your oxygen mask first and take care of yourself. But how do you do that? Increasing your positivity ratio can be done by decreasing negativity or increasing positivity.

Decreasing Negativity

Although some negativity can help us keep "grounded, real, and honest," too much negativity in our life or in a situation can have the opposite effect (Fredrickson, 2011, pg. 159). Take a few minutes and think about this question: How could you limit the amount of negativity in your life? For example, reducing the amount of negativity can be accomplished by limiting negative media influences, limiting time spent with negative people, and disputing unhelpful or negative thinking patterns. I will discuss disputing unhelpful thinking in further detail later in this part.

Increasing Positivity

Another way to increase your positivity ratio is to increase positivity in your life. For example, genuinely and sincerely experiencing some of the ten positive emotions mentioned above will be beneficial to your ratio.

Find the Silver Lining

Finding the silver lining in a situation involves finding the good within the bad, or the positive within the negative. Although it may seem difficult at times, it is always possible to find some positive meaning. The good thing is that your goal is *not* to try to take away all negativity in a situation but to redefine parts of the situation as more positive. For example, if you have had a roaring verbal argument with a teen, a silver lining in the clouds could be…"at least he or she is talking to me" (See Chapter 6).

Exercise: Notice the Silver Lining

Objective: To practice finding the "silver lining" in a conversation with a teen.

Instructions: Think back to a conversation with a teen that you felt was negative. What can you define as the "silver lining" in that conversation?

Self-reflection

- How did the exercise go?
- In what way is this important to you?
- What would you like to continue doing more of?

Exercise: Good Things

Objective: To practice focusing on the good things that happen each day.

Instructions: Reflect by yourself or together with someone you trust about the good things that have happened in your day. Commit to doing this every night before you go to sleep and see if it makes a difference in your positivity.

Self-reflection

- How did the exercise go?
- How did it make you feel when you did this?
- In what way is this important to you?
- What would you like to continue doing more of?

My husband and I try to remember to do "good things" before we go to bed. We each say three good things about our own day or ourselves, one good thing about the other person, and one good thing about each kid (we have two teens in the house now). Now that we added a puppy to our family, we have added in one good thing about the dog too ☺.

Sometimes if you've had a bad day and you have trouble coming up with something "good," remember that these are the days that you probably need it the most.

Sometimes good things may be easy to spot and sometimes they may be more difficult to recognize. That is OK. Sometimes when my husband and I do "good things," my good thing is that we tried to do it. I mean, it would have been easy to just skip doing "good things" at all. Begin to notice the small things. For example, the shining sun, a beautiful flower, the kind stranger that opened the door for you when you had your hands full, a situation that went better than expected, and so on.

Savour the Gold Lining

Finding the gold lining in the clouds involves savouring a positive situation by exploring its' positivity in greater detail. In other words, this involves appreciating and enjoying a positive situation at the time it happens.

Exercise: Past Successes

Objective: To thoroughly explore a successful situation from your past.

Instructions: Think back to a successful situation in your life that you feel positive about. It can be any situation that turned out better than you expected, a positive time in your life, a good conversation with a teen, a time when you felt proud of yourself, for example. Reflect on that situation using some of the questions below.

- What did you do or think to make this situation a success?
- How did you notice that you were successful?
- How are things different today because you were successful?
- What did you realize, learn, or discover about yourself?

Self-reflection

- How did the exercise go?
- In what way can you benefit from using this way of thinking?
- How could you incorporate this into your daily life?

Showing Kindness

Did you know that kindness and positivity feed off each other? A person's positivity ratio increases by being aware of their acts of kindness towards others. Interestingly, timing is important when increasing positivity. Research shows that performing several acts of kindness in a single day each week helps keep the feelings associated with your acts fresh, as opposed to routine (Fredrickson, 2011). So, the message here is to continue being kind every day but pick one day to do a little extra, more than normal.

Exercise: Showing Kindness[6]

Objective: To boost your own positivity by performing acts of kindness.

Instructions: Consider which acts of kindness those around you might need. For example, mow a neighbour's lawn, send a hot meal to an elderly person, or donate blood. Be creative and try to find something that would really make a difference. Choose one day a week to perform five new acts of kindness over a few months and assess how this makes you feel.

---

[6] This exercise is one of my favourite exercises for increasing positivity and can be found in Fredrickson's tool kit (Fredrickson, 2011). For more exercises for increasing positivity, see the book *The How of Happiness* by Sonja Lyubomirsky.

Self-reflection

- How did performing your acts of kindness each week make you feel?

- How has your acts of kindness affected your personal connection with that person?

- What difference has this made in your life?

Chapter Wrap-Up

Isn't it interesting that increasing positivity in your life is about much more than just trying to be positive? Chapter 12 talked about:

- The theory of positive emotions and how this can support you and your self-care.

- How to decrease negativity and increase positivity in your life.

- Finding the silver lining and its importance to you.

- Learning how to savour the gold lining in a positive situation.

- How performing acts of kindness helps you to feel better and increases your own positivity.

Chapter 13

BREATHING AND RELAXATION TECHNIQUES

*W*hen you are feeling stressed, anxious, angry, or wound up, where do you notice your breathing? Are you breathing deeply in your stomach or are you taking shallower breaths in your upper chest?

When we are relaxed and calm, our breath is in our diaphragm and stomach. When we experience strong feelings such as stress, anxiety, or anger, our body automatically reacts as if we are in danger. Our heart beats faster, our muscles tense up, and our body prepares to fight or flee.

Developing proper breathing and relaxation techniques can be very helpful ways of taking care of yourself. Breathing and relaxation techniques can help calm you and send signals throughout your body that bring relief and relaxation. Developing these skills takes time and practice. Don't give up if you don't "feel" anything the first few times.

 It may be useful to start practicing these exercises in calm situations and then employing them in more difficult situations.

Breathing Techniques

Box breathing, also called square breathing, is a breathing technique used when taking slow, deep breaths. It can heighten performance and concentration, as well as help reduce stress, worry, and anxiety (Gotter, 2020).

Exercise: Box Breathing

 **Objective:** To increase your self-care, well-being, and relaxation by reducing physical tension and feelings of stress and worry in your body.

Instructions: Sit up straight in a chair and relax your whole body. Focus on anything square-shaped to help you with this exercise (i.e., a window, piece of paper, or a photo on the wall), or if you prefer to close your eyes for this exercise, simply imagine a square in your mind. Begin the exercise by slowly exhaling all the air from your lungs.

Step 1: Breathe in deeply and slowly as your gaze follows the left side of the square from bottom to top. Count to four.

Step 2: Hold your breath and slowly allow your gaze to follow the top line, from left to right. Count to four.

Step 3: Slowly exhale and allow your gaze to follow the right side of the box from top to bottom. Count to four.

Step 4: Hold your breath again and allow your gaze to follow the bottom line of the box from right to left. Count to four.

Repeat and continue for as long as you need.

Self-reflection

- How did the exercise go?
- How did the exercise affect your body? Did it make you feel more tense or more relaxed?
- In what way can you benefit from using breathing techniques?
- When can you incorporate this into your daily routine?

Relaxation Exercises

Relaxation techniques are useful in many situations especially in situations where you feel anxious, angry, scared, or stressed. Relaxation techniques can help you unwind, feel calmer, and decrease the effects of stress on your mind and body. The exercises presented below can be practiced at any time or in any place and do not require any special accessories or aids.

Exercise: Floating Leaves on a Moving Stream[7]

Objective: To test a relaxation exercise intended to increase your well-being and relaxation by reducing physical tension.

Instructions: Follow along with the relaxation exercise detailed below.

Imagine a beautiful slow-moving stream. The water flows over the rocks, around trees, descends downhill, and travels through a valley. Once in a while, a big leaf drops into the stream and floats away down the river. Imagine you are sitting beside that stream on a warm, sunny day, watching the leaves float by.

Now become conscious of your thoughts. Each time a thought pops into your head, imagine that it is written on one of those leaves. If you think in words, put them on the leaf as words. If you think in images, put them on the leaf as an image. The goal is to stay beside the stream and allow the leaves on the stream to keep flowing by. Don't try to make the stream go faster or slower; don't try to change what shows up on the leaves in any way. If the leaves disappear, or if you mentally go somewhere else, or if you find that you are in the stream or on a leaf, just stop and notice that this happened. File that knowledge away and

---

[7] This relaxation exercise is borrowed with permission from Steven Hayes and Spencer Smith's book on Acceptance and Commitment Therapy and is one of my favourite visualization exercises for relaxation. .

then once again return to the stream, watch a thought come into your mind, write it on a leaf, and let the leaf float away down the stream.

Self-reflection

- How did the exercise go?
- How did the exercise affect your body? Did it make you feel more tense or more relaxed?
- In what way can you benefit from using relaxation techniques?
- When can you incorporate this exercise into your daily routine?

Exercise: Be Where You Are[8]

Objective: To test a relaxation exercise intended to help you be relaxed and in the present.

Instructions: Follow along with the relaxation exercise detailed below.

Find a comfortable position. You can be seated in a chair or lying down on the floor or your bed. Close your eyes and take a few deep breaths. Relax. Don't let yourself drift off to sleep but allow your body to rest.

Now slowly bring your awareness to the tips of your fingers. Feel your fingers. Rub your fingertips together. How do they feel? Can you feel the small indentations on your fingertips that are your fingerprints? Take your time and try to feel them. What are they like? Are your fingertips rough from lots of work or are the smooth and silky? How does it feel to rub them together? Notice the feeling and then move on.

---

[8] This relaxation exercise is borrowed with permission from Steven Hayes and Spencer Smith's book on Acceptance and Commitment Therapy and is one of my favourite exercises to help be in the present. .

Now rest your fingers where they were before. What are they touching? Are they resting on the blanket on your bed, or are they resting on the arm of your chair? What does that feel like? Is it soft or hard? Does it have any other distinguishing features? Is the blanket furry with cotton? Does the armrest have any markings or is it smooth? Take the time to completely absorb the way these objects feel to your fingertips.

Now bring your attention to your hands and arms. What do they feel like? Perhaps they are relaxed and heavy. Perhaps they are still tense from a long day's work. Either way is ok. There is no need to judge, simply observe the feelings in your arms and hands. Are there any aches or pains? Take note of these, but do not fixate on them. Simply note the pain and move on.

Move your attention down to your toes. Wiggle them around a little. Are they in shoes or socks? Are they free to move about? Squish your toes back and forth feeling whatever is beneath them. How does it feel? Can you tell what it is just by the feeling? Would you be able to tell by touch? Just notice the sensation as you bring your awareness to your feet.

How is your head positioned? If you are sitting, is your head aligned with your spine or is it drooping, resting on your chest? Without trying to change the position of your head, simply note where it is positioned. There is no right way for your head to be. Just let it be where it is. Now think about the sensation in your head. Do you have a headache? Is your head relaxed?

What about your face? How does your face feel? There are all kinds of sensations to explore on your face. Think about your brow. Is it smooth and flat or is it crinkled up with stress? Again, don't try to change it, just notice it. Now bring your awareness to your nose. Can you breathe freely or are you plugged up? Take a few breaths in and out through your nose. How does that feel? Can you feel cool air flowing into your lungs or is the air warm? Pay attention to the feeling for a moment. Then think about your mouth. How is your mouth positioned? Is it pursed? Is it open? Is it closed? What about the inside of your mouth? Is it wet or dry? Can you feel your saliva coat the inside of your mouth and throat? Explore all of these sensations throughout your face. Perhaps you can feel oil on your skin. Perhaps your skin is dry. Perhaps there is no feeling at all. Just note it and move on.

Now bring your attention to your chest and belly. Place one hand on your chest and one hand on your belly. Can you feel yourself breathing? What is it like? Are you breathing fast or slow? Are your breaths going into your abdomen or into your chest? Breath in through your nose and out through your mouth. How does that feel? Now invert the pattern. Spend some time with your breath, then place your hands wherever they were before.

Now think of your whole body. Where are you sitting or lying? Can you feel the backside of your body touch the chair or bed in various places? Be mindful of the way your body is positioned. There is no need to move, just observe.

Now think about the room you are in. Where are you positioned in the room? Do you have a sense of where the door is? What about the ceiling? Can you feel your body in the context of this larger space?

When you are ready, open your eyes and take a look around the room. You can move if you wish. Notice where the various pieces or furniture are. What do they look like? You can spend as much time as you like investigating the different aspects of the furniture. Remember not to judge, just notice. Whenever you are ready, you can stop this exercise and carry on with your day.

Self-reflection

- How did the exercise go?
- How did the exercise affect your body? Did it make you feel more tense or more relaxed?
- In what way can you benefit from using relaxation techniques?
- When can you incorporate this exercise into your daily routine?

Exercise: Three-minute Breathing Space meditation

Objective: To test a relaxation exercise intended to help you become relaxed and in the present moment.

Instructions: Follow along with the relaxation exercise detailed below.

Step 1: be aware

Sit upright or stand straight. If you feel comfortable doing so, close your eyes. Turn your focus inwards and be aware of your internal experiences and acknowledge them by asking yourself: What is my experience right now?

- What *thoughts* are going through the mind? Try to see your thoughts as mental events.
- What *feelings* are here? Turn towards any sense of discomfort or unpleasant feelings, noticing them without trying to change them.
- What *bodily* sensations are here right now? Scan your body for any sensations of tightness or stress, acknowledging the sensations, not trying to change them in any way.

Step 2: gather and focus your attention

Now, focus on your breathing and the physical sensations in your stomach. Notice as your diaphragm expands as you breathe in and compresses as you breathe out. Follow your breath all the way in and all the way out. Use each breath to anchor yourself in the now. If your mind wanders, that's okay. Gently guide your attention back to your breathing.

Step 3: expand your attention

Now, expand your awareness so that it includes your entire body. If you notice any bodily sensations of discomfort, tension, or stress, feel free to focus a little extra on that part of the body by imagining that the breath could move into and out of the sensation. By doing this, you are exploring the sensations and accepting them, rather than trying to change them in any way.

Self-reflection

- How did the exercise go?
- How did the exercise affect your body? Did it make you feel more tense or more relaxed?
- In what way can you benefit from using relaxation techniques?
- When can you incorporate this exercise into your daily routine?

Chapter Wrap-Up

Breathing and relaxation techniques can help calm you and send signals throughout your body that bring relief and relaxation. These signals benefit your ability to communicate more effectively with a teen. Chapter 13 presented:

- The technique of box breathing and its benefits.
- A relaxation and visualization exercise based on Acceptance Commitment Therapy (ACT)[9].
- Two relaxation exercises to help you become grounded and be mindful in the present.

---

[9] For more information on exercises in acceptance, try reading Hayes & Smith's book *Get Out of Your Mind & Into Your Life. The New Acceptance & Commitment Therapy.*

Chapter 14

COPING WITH STRONG FEELINGS

Our Basic Emotions

*R*esearchers studying emotions agree on five basic human emotions that are shared by all people regardless of how or where they are raised. The basic human emotions – anger, fear, disgust, sadness, and happiness – vary in strength and frequency, and from moment to moment (Ekman, 1992).

We have all experienced variations of these five basic human emotions at some point in our lives, even during our interactions and conversations with teens. Our basic emotions are necessary and serve an important purpose. If we pay attention to and acknowledge our emotions, they let us know how we are feeling in a situation, help us understand and modify our current actions, and guide our behaviour in the future. We also tend to categorize and judge these normal emotional states, for example as positive or negative depending on their level of pleasantry which can affect our thinking in certain situations.

Throughout our lives, and sometimes daily, we can experience a roller coaster of these emotions and can benefit from noticing, identifying, and accepting what we are feeling at any given moment. But how can we do that?

Exercise: Accepting your Emotions

Objective: To test an exercise intended to help you cope with a difficult situation by accepting any thoughts, feelings, and bodily sensations that may have arisen.

Instructions: Follow along with the relaxation exercise detailed below.

Follow along at a pace that you feel comfortable with. Allow your breathing to help anchor you within the moment. Identify whereabouts in your body, your breathing is most noticeable to you within this moment. Concentrate your attention there and focus on how you are breathing without changing it in any way. Use your breathing to help you stay in that moment.

Now think of a difficult situation that you have experienced. Imagine this situation clearly in your mind. Allow all the emotions and thoughts brought up by this situation to be reawakened and just bubble and appear at the surface.

In this difficult situation, how are you feeling? What emotions are you experiencing in this difficult situation?

(Pause)

When you imagine that you are in this difficult situation, how does your body feel? What bodily sensations become more noticeable to you or change?

(Pause)

And when you imagine that you are in this difficult situation, what thoughts come to you? What thoughts come to you in this difficult situation? How do these thoughts affect you?

Choose now to accept everything you become aware of. Accept them with your entire self - your heart, mind, and body. Express your acceptance quietly to yourself.

I choose to accept this even if I don't like it.

I choose to accept these feelings even if I don't like them.

I choose to accept these bodily sensations even if I don't like them.

I choose to accept these thoughts even if I don't like them.

(Pause)

Repeat this quietly over and over to yourself.

(Pause)

I choose to have this even if I don't like it.

Concentrate on your breathing for a couple of breaths at your own pace – in and out.

Now take a deep breath and slowly open your eyes.

Self-reflection

- How did the exercise go?
- How did the exercise affect your body? Did it make you feel more tense or more relaxed?
- In what way can you benefit from using relaxation techniques?
- When can you incorporate this exercise into your daily routine?

Emotion Surfing

Every so often, we experience emotions that we consider extremely uncomfortable. When this happens, our instinct is to do whatever we can to protect ourselves by avoiding unpleasant emotions or alleviating and removing them. We get ready to fight these unpleasantries when accepting them could prove more successful.

One way of coping with unpleasant emotions is to imagine feeling the emotion as if surfing a wave, known as emotion surfing (McKay & West, 2016). Emotion surfing involves observing uncomfortable feelings with genuine curiosity and accepting an unpleasant emotional experience, without reacting to it (i.e., judging it), trying to control it, or attempting to change it. The aim of emotion surfing is to *describe* an emotional experience and become aware of any distressful thoughts.

Emotion surfing helps us to objectively look at our thoughts and feelings, to become aware of different ways of reacting to the current situation and allows us to choose how we would like to handle the situation. It encourages us to realize and accept that our thoughts and emotions come and go like waves. Due to this, it helps us understand that our thoughts do not define us or our actions and that we can choose which thoughts to pay attention to and act upon and which thoughts to ignore. When you increase your emotional awareness, you increase your ability to take control over your behaviour. Emotion surfing[10] is a skill that can be learned and perfected through practice. It requires openness and courage to welcome, observe, and accept unpleasant feelings.

Exercise: Emotion Surfing

Objective: To test an exercise in emotion surfing, intended to help you cope with a difficult situation.

Instructions: Follow along with the relaxation exercise detailed below and try to accept any thoughts, feelings, and bodily sensations that may arise.

---

[10] More information on emotion surfing can be found in McKay & West's book *Emotion Efficacy Therapy. A Brief, Exposure-Based Treatment for Emotion Regulation Integrating ACT & DBT* or on the following website: https://www.newharbinger.com/blog/teaching-clients-art-emotion-surfing-through-mindful-acceptance.

Sit comfortably with your hands resting on your lap. Take a few deep breaths and close your eyes. Then focus your attention inwards and observe your bodily sensations. Be aware of your bodily sensations within that moment.

Imagine yourself in a situation where you have experienced, or are currently experiencing, unpleasant emotions (i.e., anger, irritation, sadness, anxiety).

When you have that situation clear in your mind, try to recognize the unpleasant emotion you are experiencing and embrace it. At the same time, be aware of your breathing. Observe and identify where you feel the emotion in your body. Experience this feeling like a wave coming towards you. Breathe deeply into the wave as it approaches. As the wave flows away from you, breathe out. Resist the urge to relieve your unpleasant emotion by "surfing" it.

Try to describe to yourself what you are experiencing. If any other thoughts or sounds appear in your consciousness, make a mental note of them but don't dwell on them, and then return your attention to your breathing.

Continue to breathe deeply and observe what is happening in your body.

During this exercise, answer the following questions quietly to yourself:

- Did the feeling wander around your body or did it stay in the same place?
- Was the feeling constant or did it come and go, or vary in strength?
- Did you become hotter or colder?
- Were your muscles tense or relaxed?

- If you were to describe the feeling with a picture, what would it look like?

When you have answered the last question to yourself, slowly open your eyes.

Self-reflection

- How did the exercise go?
- How did the exercise affect your body? Did it make you feel more tense or more relaxed?
- In what way can you benefit from using this technique?
- When can you incorporate this exercise into your daily routine?

Chapter Wrap-Up

Human emotions are a fact of life and affect how we interact and communicate with others. This chapter covered:

- The five basic human emotions, which are fear, happiness, anger, disgust, and sadness.
- The importance of becoming aware of, acknowledging, and accepting your feelings in a particular situation.
- The idea of emotion surfing and its positive impact on your well-being.

Chapter 15

BEING KIND TO YOURSELF

As mentioned above, kindness and positivity feed off each other. If performing acts of kindness help you to feel better and increase positivity, then it is also just as important to show yourself kindness, compassion, and acceptance. Doing things that increase your well-being (i.e., thinking positively about yourself) is a great way to provide yourself with emotional and psychological self-care. Below is the link to a video by a colleague of mine, Dr. Stan Steindl, a psychologist specializing in the art of being kind to yourself. Take some time to watch his video for a great introduction to self-compassion. You can find the video at https://en.novovia.se/bookresources.[11]

Exercise: Discovering your Personal Attributes

Objective: To familiarize yourself with and practice recognizing your own personal qualities and attributes.

Instructions: Reflect on and answer the questions below to familiarize and recognize your own personal qualities and attributes.

- Which qualities or attributes do you value in others?
- Of those qualities or attributes, which do you possess yourself?

---

[11] For more information on self-compassion, feel free to check out Stan's book "The Gifts of Compassion."

- Of those qualities or attributes, which do you wish you possessed? What are your reasons for wishing for that?
- Describe yourself using five adjectives.
- What do you think are your best qualities or attributes?
- When was the last time you used …(quality or attribute)…?
- Which aspects of yourself do you like the most?
- What are you good at? What is it that makes you good at it?

Self-reflection

- How did the exercise go?
- How did completing the exercise make you feel?
- In what way can you benefit from using this way of thinking?
- When can you incorporate this into your daily routine?

Exercise: Affirming Yourself

 **Objective:** To practice giving positive feedback or affirmations to yourself as a way of taking care of yourself.

Instructions: Pay attention to the positives within yourself and practice giving yourself positive feedback or affirmations every day. You could do this by writing your affirmations in a journal or by speaking them out loud, perhaps when standing in front of a mirror. Feel free to affirm yourself using the acronym **VASE**: **V**alues, **A**ttributes, **S**trengths/resources, **E**fforts.

 The art of affirming is a way of acknowledging a person's strengths and efforts, including your own. Feel free to revisit Chapter 8 for a detailed explanation of affirmation.

V – What values or priorities can you see?

A – What qualities or attributes are evident within you?

S – What strengths do you see in yourself?

E – What effort(s) are you making?

Self-reflection

- How did the exercise go? How did completing it make you feel?

- In what way can you benefit from affirming yourself?

- How can you incorporate this into your daily routine?

Chapter Wrap-Up

Kindness and positivity feed off each other so showing yourself kindness is a big part of taking care of yourself. This chapter covered:

- The importance of showing yourself compassion and acceptance.

- The importance of thinking positively about yourself.

- How to see the positives within yourself and affirm yourself using VASE (Values, Attributes, Strengths/resources, Efforts).

Chapter 16

SOCIAL AND EMOTIONAL SELF-CARE

Engaging in Meaningful Leisure Time

Obtaining, maintaining, and engaging in meaningful leisure activities is an important aspect of self-care. When we are feeling down, stressed, or anxious, we often stop doing the things that work to counteract that negativity. Therefore, it is crucial when you are feeling down to continue to engage in the activities that make you feel good and nourish you during your leisure time.

Exercise: Nourishing your Leisure Time

Objective: To demonstrate kindness towards yourself by nourishing your leisure time.

Instructions: Reflect on the things (i.e., people or activities) that make you feel good and increase your well-being. This can include but is not limited to reading a book, going for a walk, catching up with a friend or family member, meditating, playing a musical instrument, and so on. Commit to doing one of these things each day and reflect on how this action has affected your mood.

Self-reflection

- How did the exercise go?
- What acts of kindness did you perform for yourself?

- How did nourishing your leisure time make you feel?
- In what way can this be beneficial to you?
- How can you incorporate this into your daily life?

Your Basic Need for Relatedness

Central to Self-determination Theory (SDT) is the idea that all humans have basic psychological needs that affect their psychological growth and well-being. SDT focuses on how three basic psychological needs (autonomy, relatedness, and competence) influence their choices and behaviour (Deci & Ryan 1985, 2012). *Relatedness* refers to our evolutionary and psychological needs for belonging and to our need to feel connected with others. We need to be a part of a social community, to feel loved and valued in a social environment (See Chapter 5). By engaging in social and emotional self-care, you aim to satisfy your basic need for relatedness.

We are, by nature, social beings and need people around us – friends, family, and acquaintances – who are there for us and who can support us. Feeling genuinely cared for, listened to, understood, and loved makes it much easier to cope in difficult and stressful situations. Social and emotional support from others can also include practical help or information. Having a support system of people you can trust and count on, and who nourish these relationships can be an example of social and emotional self-care.

Exercise: Nourishing your Relationships

Objective: To take care of and nourish the relationships that are important to you.

Instructions: Reflect on the following questions and choose to actively do something to nourish your relationships. For example, you may decide to send an email, text message, card in the mail or connect via telephone or online program (i.e., Facetime, Zoom, Skype).

- Which relationships are important to you?
- What can you do to nourish these relationships?

Self-reflection

- Which relationship did you choose to nourish?
- What reason(s) did you have for choosing that relationship?
- What did you do to nourish that relationship?
- What response did you get from the other person?
- How did this make you feel?
- How could you incorporate this into your daily life?

Exercise: Showing Appreciation

Objective: To show appreciation for someone in your network.

Instructions: Consider the people in your private or professional network. Reflect on what you appreciate and value within them. Reflect upon what it means to you to have them in your life. Decide how you would like to express your appreciation to them (i.e., send a card, text message, or email, make a telephone call, or meet over a cup of coffee). Take the time and express your appreciation to them.

Self-reflection

- Which person did you choose to express your appreciation for?
- What reason(s) did you have for choosing that person?
- How did you express your appreciation? What did you say?

- In what way has this nourished that relationship?
- What response did you get from the other person?
- How did this make you feel?
- How can you incorporate this into your daily life?

Asking for Help

People are often willing, ready, and able to help their friends, family, and acquaintances. However, those in your social network may not always know when or that you need support and help. Although it can be difficult, it is important to remember that you are not alone and be able to ask for support when you need it the most. The following exercise provides you with four steps to use to ask for help when you find it difficult. The steps are developed by Goldstein, Glick & Gibbs (1998).

Exercise: Asking for Help

Objective: To ask someone in your network for help.

Instructions: Practice asking someone in your network for help by using the following steps.

1. Decide what the problem is. Clearly define the problem you are facing which needs to be resolved.
2. Decide if you want help with the problem. Do you need help? What are the advantages and disadvantages of asking for help?
3. Think about different people who might help you and pick one. Make a list of all the people who may be able to help you and choose the one that you feel may be the best one.
4. Tell the person about the problem and ask that person for help.

Self-reflection

- How did it feel to ask for help?
- What was the other person's response?
- Did you use the steps above? How did it feel to use them?
- In what way can you benefit from using these steps?
- When can you incorporate this into your daily life?

Chapter Wrap-Up

Humans are social beings, and it is important to take care of yourself both socially and emotionally. Obtaining, maintaining, and engaging in meaningful leisure activities is an important aspect of self-care. In doing so you satisfy your own basic need for *relatedness*. This chapter focused on:

- The value of nourishing your leisure time and doing the things that make you feel good.
- The importance of feeling genuinely cared for, listened to, understood, and loved.
- Having a support system of people around you and nourishing those relationships.
- Showing appreciation for people in your social and professional networks can improve your own well-being.
- The idea of asking for help and how you can go about doing that.

Chapter 17

DEVELOPING HELPFUL THINKING PATTERNS

*T*he brain is a truly amazing organ. As mentioned earlier in the book, the pre-frontal cortex is responsible for comprehension, decision-making, considering consequences, planning, problem-solving, and handling strong emotions (See Chapter 2). This means that we humans think – a LOT! And that also means that we have a lot of thoughts, some of which are very helpful, some of which are very unhelpful, and some of which are somewhere in-between, in a grey zone. And our thoughts about a specific situation are connected to and affect both our feelings and behaviour (see picture). Usually, this is not an issue when our thoughts are "helpful" (or positive) as they generally affect our emotions and behaviour in a positive way. However, thoughts that are "unhelpful" (or negative) often arise automatically or unconsciously and affect our emotions and behaviour negatively, thus making them more difficult to tackle.

Tackling and reducing unhelpful or negative thoughts is at the heart of Cognitive Behavioural Therapy (CBT). By increasing awareness of automatic, "unhelpful" or negative thoughts,

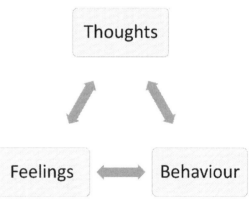

we can challenge and modify them into more "helpful" or positive thoughts, that increase our well-being and help us to constructively handle difficult situations.

Exercise: Being Aware of "Helpful" or Positive Thoughts

Objective: To be aware of your "helpful" or positive thoughts and how these thoughts can affect your feelings and behaviour.

Instructions: Reflect on a situation that you feel good about. Try to remember this situation as clearly as possible. Use the following questions to guide your own self-reflection.

- What feelings are associated with this situation?
- What thoughts went through your head?
- How did you act? What did you say?

Self-reflection

- What insights did the exercise give you?
- In what way can you benefit from it?
- When can you incorporate this into your daily routine?

Exercise: Tackling "Unhelpful" or Negative Thoughts
Part One: Increasing awareness

Objective: To increase awareness of your "unhelpful" or negative thoughts and how these thoughts affect your feelings and behaviour.

Instructions: Reflect on a challenging or difficult situation that you have had with a teen within your circle. For example, an interaction or conversation with a teen that you did not feel good about or did not go as you had hoped or planned. Try to remember this situation as clearly as possible. Use the following questions and/or the table provided below to help guide your self-reflection.

- What feelings are associated with this situation?
- What thoughts went through your head immediately before, during, and after the interaction?
- How did you behave immediately before, during, and after the interaction?

Situation	Before	During	After
Feelings			
Thoughts			
Behaviour (actions and words)			

 Remember the five basic human emotions – anger, fear, disgust, sadness, and happiness (See Chapter 14).

Part Two: Increasing Awareness of the Consequences of Your Thoughts

Objective: To reflect on some of the consequences of your "unhelpful" or negative thoughts.

Instructions: Look at the "unhelpful" or negative thoughts discovered in part one. Reflect on the consequences of these thoughts with the help of the questions below and/or use the table below to write down your answers.

- How did your "unhelpful" or negative thoughts affect your behaviour, feelings, and other thoughts?
- What are some of the consequences resulting from your "unhelpful" or negative thoughts?
- Which consequences are positive or negative? Which consequences have short-term and/or long-term effects?
- Other than you, who is/are affected by these consequences?

"Unhelpful" Thought	Consequences		
		Short-term	Long-term
	Positive		
	Negative		

Part Three: Challenging Your Thoughts

Once you have become aware of and identified your "unhelpful" or negative thoughts, and considered the consequences of these thoughts, you are now ready to tackle them by challenging their existence and usefulness.

Objective: To challenge your "unhelpful" or negative thoughts.

Instructions: Look at the "unhelpful" or negative thoughts discovered in part one. Challenge each of your "unhelpful" thoughts using some of the techniques presented below.

- What evidence/proof is there that your thought is accurate?
- What are the advantages and disadvantages of thinking this way?

- If this was someone else's thought, what would you think about it?
- How likely is it that your thought is correct?
- What other possible explanations could there be for your thought?
- Will this matter in 5 minutes, 5 weeks, 5 months, or in 5 years?

Part Four: Put it all Together

Objective: To increase awareness for your "unhelpful" or negative thinking, explore the consequences of your thinking, and challenge your "unhelpful" thoughts.

Instructions: Think of another challenging or difficult situation with a teen and use the following table to first identify your "unhelpful" or negative thoughts and then challenge them.

"Unhelpful" thought	Consequences	Challenge it!

Self-reflection

- What insights did the exercises give you?
- In what way can you benefit from them?
- When can you incorporate these into your daily routine?

Replacing "Unhelpful" Thoughts

Another way of tackling and reducing your "unhelpful" or negative thoughts is to consider replacing them with more "helpful" ones. This is an effective way to affect or change your feelings and behaviour. Consider the examples below.

"Unhelpful" (or negative) thoughts	"Helpful" (or positive) thoughts
What are your "unhelpful" thoughts?	What thought(s) might be more helpful for you to think of instead? What could you replace your "unhelpful" thoughts with?
Example: *"He's just arguing and picking a fight with me, he's just testing me."*	Example: *"He feels safe with me in our relationship, so safe that he feels comfortable to test me/it. This is normal behaviour for a teen, and it will pass. I just need to stay calm."*
Example: *"Her impulsivity always gets her into trouble."*	Example: *"She really is a brave and curious girl."*

Exercise: Replacing "Unhelpful" Thoughts

Objective: To practice replacing your "unhelpful" or negative thoughts with more "helpful" or positive ones.

Instructions: Look back at the "unhelpful" or negative thoughts from part one of the previous exercise (Exercise: Tackling "Unhelpful" or Negative Thoughts). Write them down in the table below and try to replace them with more positive and helpful thoughts. Feel free to write down your "unhelpful" and replacement thoughts using the table below.

"Unhelpful" (or negative) thoughts	"Helpful" (or positive) thoughts
What are your "unhelpful thoughts?"	What thought(s) might be more helpful for you to think of instead? What could you replace your unhelpful thoughts with?

Self-reflection

- What insights did the exercise give you?
- In what way can you benefit from it?
- When can you incorporate this into your daily routine?

Chapter Wrap-Up

This chapter was dedicated to how your thoughts, feelings, and behaviours affect your relationships and communications with a teen in your circle. It covered:

- Increasing awareness for both your helpful and "unhelpful" thoughts.
- How to tackle and reduce "unhelpful" or negative thinking patterns.
- Recognizing the consequences of your "unhelpful" thoughts.
- The process of challenging and replacing "unhelpful" thoughts with helpful thoughts.

Chapter 18

CONCLUSION

*B*y using Motivational Interviewing (MI), you create the conditions that are essential for developing and enriching a positive relationship with a teen in your circle. Using the tools presented in *Lighthouse Conversations* will make communication with teens more effective. The book covered listening skills needed for good communication, the importance of understanding and exploring a teen's inner motivation for change, the cornerstones of MI ("team spirit", compassion, acceptance, a positive focus). The framework and tool EOE: Explore-Offer-Explore was presented as a way for you to listen to and understand a teen's perspective. EOE helps you to package and respectfully deliver your message in a way that helps the teen internalize it. EOE aims to support and promote the teen's need for autonomy and increases the teen's motivation to do things differently in the future. *Lighthouse Conversations* also provided you with the theory, means, and tools to do the following in your future conversations with teens.

- Handle situations where your "righting reflex" is prominent, and you may be wearing your "expert hat."
- Build "team spirit" between you and the teen (have a *team* focus).
- Show compassion and focus on the teen's needs in a particular moment (a *teen* focus).

- Put on your "positive eye-glasses" (have a *positive* focus) and strive to recognize, identify, explore, and verbalize the teen's internal strengths and resources (affirm the teen).

- Convey empathy and try to understand the teen's perspective.

- Show acceptance for the teen's need for self-determination and autonomy.

- Support and promote the teen's autonomy.

- Recognize and encourage a teen's own reasons for change (change talk).

- Take care of yourself, physically, emotionally, and psychologically, to be able to communicate effectively with a teen.

QUIZ ANSWER CODE KEYS

Quiz: Identifying Change Talk (pages 36-37) - Answer Key

1. Conversational context or focus: Take care of the family pet.

   "I'll take the dog for a walk when I get home from school." (Change Talk)

2. Conversational context or focus: School work.

   "I hope I get a better grade on this test." (Change Talk)

3. Conversational context or focus: Make it to school on time.

   "I might make it to school on time if I went to bed earlier." (Change Talk)

4. Conversational context or focus: Handle feelings of depression.

   "I cannot keep feeling like this. I need to talk to someone who can help me." (Change Talk)

5. Conversational context or focus: Improve a relationship with a parent.

   "I am prepared to try." (Change Talk)

6. Conversational context or focus: Get a job.

   "Yesterday, I went to three places about a summer job." (Change Talk)

7. Conversational context or focus: Quit smoking.

   "I love smoking. It makes me look cool" (not Change Talk)

8. Conversational context or focus: Do school work.

"I just need to accept that I am stupid. That's just the way it is." (not Change Talk)

9. Conversational context or focus: Do school work.

"I would way rather be with my friends than doing school work." (not Change Talk)

10. Conversational context or focus: Handle a situation without violence.

"If I beat her up, then I will probably get suspended or something." (Change Talk)

11. Conversational context or focus: Handle a situation without violence.

"Someone has to teach him a lesson!" (not Change Talk)

12. Conversational context or focus: Refrain from drinking at a party.

"Absolutely not! Are you crazy?" (not Change Talk)

Quiz: Recognizing the Change Talk (page 38) - Answer Key

Change talk / not change talk

1. Conversational context or focus: Help with chores.

   "I'm sorry. *I'd like to help you with the laundry,* but I just don't have the time."

2. Conversational context or focus: Continue engaging in a sport.

   "*I used to like going* to basketball practice but it's just not fun anymore."

3. Conversational context or focus: Working out a conflict.

   "Janet is my best friend, but she just isn't treating me very nicely. I guess *I should talk to her* about it."

4. Conversational context or focus: Quit smoking.

   "It's *pretty expensive to smoke* but there are always ways to bum cigarettes off people."

5. Conversational context or focus: Handle anxiety.

   "I suppose *it might help to talk to a counsellor* about my anxiety but I'm not sure that I am ready."

6. Conversational context or focus: Refrain from drinking alcohol.

   "Everybody was drinking at the party this weekend and I had to be the driver. I wish I could've had fun too. But, it was so *annoying watching everyone stumble around and slur their words.*"

7. Conversational context or focus: Asking an older sibling to buy alcohol.

   "My older brother is so annoying. *I know I shouldn't have asked him* to buy me booze but he could've at least done it just this once."

Quiz: Difference Between a Positive and Negative Focus (page 58) - Answer Key

	Statement/thought	Answer key
1	"My son is always late for school"	Negative focus
2	"John is doing the best that he can do"	Positive focus
3	"Why does she always have to scream and fight at home?"	Negative focus
4	"She leaves her stuff everywhere all the time"	Negative focus
5	"I wonder what helped her get up for school today"	Positive focus
6	"He's not old enough to know what's best for him"	Negative focus
7	"You probably know what works best for you"	Positive focus
8	"He probably had some good reasons for doing what he did. I need to ask him about that later"	Positive focus
9	"I have to get her to understand that what she did was wrong!"	Negative focus
10	"I should maybe ask her for her view of the situation"	Positive focus

REFERENCES

Alberti, R. & Emmons, M. (2017). *Your Perfect Right* (10th ed). Oakland, CA: Impact Publishers.

Cole, S., Gutnick, D., Davis, C. & Reims, K. (2012). *Brief Action Planning Guide.* www.centreCMI.ca

Deci, E.L. & Ryan, R.M. (1985). *Intrinsic motivation and self-determination in human behavior.* New York: Plenum Press.

Deci, E. L., & Ryan, R. M. (2012). Motivation, personality, and development within embedded social contexts: An overview of self-determination theory. In R. M. Ryan (Ed.), *Oxford handbook of human motivation* (pp. 85-107). Oxford, UK: Oxford University Press.

Dixelius & Ljunggren (2019). *Motiverande Samtal med kodning som verktyg.* Stockholm: Gothia Fortbildning.

Dolgin, Kim Gale (2014). *The Adolescent: Development, relationships, culture* (14th ed). Essex England: Pearson Education Limited.

Fredrickson, B. (2011). *Positivity. Groundbreaking Research to Release Your Inner Optimist and Thrive.* Oxford, England: Oneworld Publications.

Gilbert, Paul, A. (2013). *The Compassionate Mind.* UK: Constable.

Glick, Barry & Gibbs, John (2011). *Aggression Replacement Training: A Comprehensive Intervention for Aggressive Youth* (3rd ed). Champaign, IL: Research Press.

Goldstein, A., Glick, B., & Gibbs, J. (1998). *Aggression Replacement Therapy: A Comprehensive Intervention for Aggressive Youth.* Illinois: Malloy Inc.

Gordon, Thomas (2019). *Parent effectiveness training (Revised Edition).* New York, NY: First Harmony.

Hayes, Steven C & Smith, Spencer. (2005). *Get Out of Your Mind & Into Your Life. The New Acceptance & Commitment Therapy.* Oakland: New Harbinger Publications.

Hwang, P. & Nilsson, B. (2011). *Utvecklingspsykologi.* Stockholm: Natur & Kultur.

Jensen, Frances E. (2015). *The Teenage Brain: A neuroscientist's survival guide to raising adolescents and young adults.* Great Britian: HarperThorsons.

Lyubomirsky, Sonja (2009). *The How of Happiness: A New Approach to Getting the Life You Want.* USA: Penguin Group.

McKay, Matthew & West, Aprilia (2016). *Emotion Efficacy Therapy. A Brief, Exposure-Based Treatment for Emotion Regulation Integrating ACT & DBT.* New Harbinger Publications: Oakland. https://www.newharbinger.com/blog/teaching-clients-art-emotion-surfing-through-mindful-acceptance

Miller, W.R. (2018). *Listening Well. The art of empathic listening.* Eugene, OR: Wipf & Stock Publishers.

Miller, William R. & Moyers, Theresa B. (2021). *Effective Psychotherapists. Clinical Skills that Improve Clients Outcomes.* New York, NY: Guilford Press.

Miller, W.R. & Rollnick, S. (2013). *Motivational Interviewing. Helping People Change.* (3rd ed). New York, NY: Guilford Press.

Naar, Sylvie & Safren, Steven A. (2017). *Motivational Interviewing and CBT. Combining Strategies for Maximum Effectiveness.* New York, NY: Guilford Press.

Naar-King, Sylvie & Suarez, Mariann (2011). *Motivational Interviewing and young adults.* New York, NY: Guilford Press.

Ortiz, L. & Skoglund, C. (2017). *Lyssnar din tonåring. Samtal med förändring som mål.* Stockholm: Natur & Kultur.

Rollnick, S., Kaplan, S. & Rutschman, R. (2016). *Motivational Interviewing in Schools.* New York, NY: Guilford Press.

Ryan, Richard M. & Deci, Edward L. (2018). *Self-Determination Theory: Basic Psychological Needs in Motivation, Development, and Wellness.* New York, NY: Guilford Press.

Smyth, Bobby. (2017, October 5-7). *Disentangling Adolescence and Substance Use* [Conference session]. MINT 2017 Forum, Malahide, Ireland.

Steindl, Stan (2020). *The Gifts of Compassion. How to Understand and Overcome Suffering.* Samford Valley: Australian Academic Press.

Williams, G.C. (2002). Improving patients' health through supporting the autonomy of patients and providers. In E.L. Deci & R.M. Ryan (Eds.), *Handbook of self-determination research* (p.233-254). Rochester, NY: University of Rochester Press.

Williams, Mark. & Penman, Danny (2011). *Mindfulness: A Practical Guide to Finding Peace in a Frantic World.* London: Piatkus.

WEBSITES

Ekman (1992). Atlas of Emotions, http://atlasofemotions.org/

Gotter, Ana (2020, June 17). *Box Breathing,* https://www.healthline.com/health/box-breathing.

Homeland Office England, https://www.crimesolutions.gov/ProgramDetails.aspx?ID=532

LaRock, Hana (2019, May 6). *What is Tentative Language?* The Classroom, Leaf Group Education. https://www.theclassroom.com/tentative-language-10051363.html

Proofreading Academy (2020). *What to do with tentative language?,* https://www.proofreadingacademy.com/advice/what-to-do-with-tentative-language/

McKay, Matthew & West, Aprilia (2016). *Emotion Efficacy Therapy. A Brief, Exposure-Based Treatment for Emotion Regulation Integrating ACT & DBT.* New Harbinger Publications: Oakland. https://www.newharbinger.com/blog/teaching-clients-art-emotion-surfing-through-mindful-acceptance.

Young, Karen (2021). *With Kids and Teens.* https://www.heysigmund.com/the-adolescent-brain-what-they-need-to-know/

ABOUT THE AUTHOR

Jennifer Ollis Blomqvist, BSc, MSW, is an inspirational, committed, and trusted expert in Motivational Interviewing (MI) with over 20 years of experience teaching and using it in organizations. Born in Canada, she earned a BSc in Psychology from the University of Alberta and a Masters in Social Work from the University of Gothenburg, completing her MI training while working in the criminal justice system in Sweden. She started her company NovoVia Consulting to train professionals in MI and compassionately guide them to adopt this alternative approach to solve serious and everyday problems. Now she is applying this success model in education to introduce MI as a proven solution for organizations and individuals to achieve long-lasting change through self-motivation.

As a Cognitive Behavioural Coach, Jennifer has extensive experience working with clients struggling with physical and psychological issues (e.g., alcohol and substance abuse, criminal behaviour, violence, victims of sexual offences, eating disorders, self-esteem, setting boundaries, impulse control). Jennifer is committed to spreading MI to benefit individuals and society by helping people and those who love them be ready for change, solve life's most challenging issues, and prevent problems from negatively impacting their lives. This book is an expression of her work and passion for helping others.

Made in the USA
Coppell, TX
05 February 2023

12272622R00118